MARIPOSA COUNTY COURTHOUSE

MARIPOSA — THE PRESENT COUNTY SEAT IN 1854
MARIPOSA GRANT

MARIPOSA COUNTY COURTHOUSE
"Shrine to Justice"

A History

by

SCOTT PINKERTON

Photography by

LEROY RADANOVICH

MARIPOSA HERITAGE PRESS

MARIPOSA, CALIFORNIA

Library of Congress Card Catalog Number 89-062410
ISBN 0-9624797-0-5

Designed by Mariposa Heritage Press

Published in cooperation with
Pioneer Publishing Co., Fresno

Mariposa Heritage Press
5038 Fairgrounds Drive
Mariposa, California 95338

Frontispiece: Charleton Watkins 1860 Salt Print of the town of Mariposa.

Dedicated to

Perrin V. Fox

and

Augustus F. Shriver

Designer and builders

of the Mariposa County Courthouse

In 1935 John Dexter, editor of the *Mariposa Gazette*, said: "Certainly the builders of the Mariposa Courthouse did honest work and used honest materials. The old courthouse certainly is a monument to the faithfulness, integrity, and honor of those pioneers who 'builded well.'"

This book resulted from their labors.

Mariposa Court House

Why throng the men at river, brook and rill
Where yesterday the sleeping land lay still,
As it had lain through timeless ages while
Its sire, the Sun, approved its dreaming smile?

'Tis gold! For also had the Sun begot
And hidden, as ashamed, that which would not
Revere the quiet vale or templed grove
Or singing waters when for it men strove.

From east, from west, from all the world they came,
By sea, o'er plain, from plow and desk, to claim
A chance in Fortune's lottery and see
Their fate remolded as they would it be.

No better they, nor worse, than those who strive
In market place or slum to stay alive
And love and breed and serve—or need be slay—
Their fellow men. So was it in that day.

But some there were, enough there were, who brought
From far-off homes respect for Law and sought
To plant it in a lawless land—among
Them one who knew that Law to Beauty clung.

An architect and builder, he aroused
The thought that Justice ever must be housed
As in a temple, pledging he would draw
And build a structure fitting for The Law.

Whereby in that rude mining camp there grew,
Pure in design and purpose, builded true,
Still serving Law, the oldest Court House used
In California—where Law lay bruised.

And Mariposa now is thronged again
By seekers—not for gold but beauty—men
And wives and progeny who daily pass
To view Yosemite, where it doth mass

Beyond their dreams of Eden, glorified
By vision of God's majesty. Beside
His ancient trees and mountain dome
They find their quest—and take it home.

Among the worshippers you will discern
The Nation's architects, who come to learn
Of God how they shall build, as did those men
With honest eye and hand who builded then.

by Duane Edwin Fox,
son of Perrin V. Fox

May 1941

Contents

Acknowledgements

To the editors of newspapers who over the years have preserved in text and pictures the day-to-day events that have become the history of this noble building, we give our "thanks" for their persistence. Also, to the many unknown photographers, and especially to our dear friend, the late Harold Rowney, for diligently capturing on film the events at the courthouse.

We also acknowledge with deep appreciation the past boards of supervisors for listening to their constituents' wishes in preserving this courthouse for those in the future to treasure and for maintaining it as the seat of county government. Also our appreciation to the Mariposa County Historical Sites and Records Preservation Commission for contributing their time in protecting the courthouse. To State Senator Ken Maddy and Assemblymen Bill Jones and Jim Costa for their letters and deeds in support of grant applications for restoration of the structure. Also to the State of California Department of Parks and Recreation and the Office of Historical Preservation for support in recognizing the need to preserve this "Shrine to Justice" for future generations.

The authors want to recognize especially those citizens who, over the years, have successfully fought to protect the architectural integrity of this edifice. This would include those with the foresight to organize the Mariposa County Historical Society, that began to preserve our cherished history.

We also acknowledge George Towne of Sunnyvale, great grandson of the designer, P. V. Fox, and the son and daughters of the late Honorable Andrew Schottky, the third superior court judge of Mariposa County, for their cooperation with our including two poems that so aptly express the feelings that we, and hopefully present and future generations, feel toward the courthouse.

To our wives, for their support, go our special thanks.

Leroy Radanovich
Scott Pinkerton

John Charles Fremont as a young man.

Introduction

"Fire!" was the urgent cry that came from the county clerk's office in the Mariposa County Courthouse just before noon on Friday, April 10, 1903. Soot in the boarded-up fireplace had caught fire, and had it not been discovered until after the noon hour, the topic of this book would have been no more.

The original building was quite small. Even when additions were constructed, the courthouse was still smaller than most in the West. For more than 135 years, it has served as the seat of justice and government in Mariposa County. While other courthouses have been replaced or torn down, this edifice has endured because of its unique architecture and the character of the people it serves.

We celebrate our good fortune in having such a useful friend by bringing to you the history of this ageless structure. In the last few years, there has been a renewed interest in making sure that future generations can share and enjoy what we most proudly possess.

Use this book as a guide, not only to the history of the wood, pegs, shingles and clock, but to the character of the citizens of Mariposa County who have found preservation of this structure preferable to its replacement. Be aware that within this simple structure the law found maturity and innovation. Principles routinely applied within the courtrooms of our nation first found expression echoing off these rough-planed walls. What giants these men must have been, to give us such gifts.

Devoid of excessive embellishments, simple of line and form, eminently flexible to the changing needs of the populace, this courthouse has served us well. While not always appreciated, even by some of its own citizens, it has engendered a growing affection far and wide as the decades have passed.

The authors consider this effort a labor of love. We hope that future generations will see this structure as more than wood and paint, and endeavor to continue to preserve this monument to our past and a beacon to our future.

1 Brief History of Mariposa County

As of this writing, a complete history or even a "mini-text" remains to be written about this southernmost county in the California gold region. The reader must surmise that many books are to be written before the history of this "Mother of Counties" will be recorded.

No attempt to account for all 139 years of Mariposa County's history will be made in this chapter. However, the reader is entitled to have a working knowledge of events leading up to and following the placement "on a high eminence" of that great edifice we so proudly refer to as "Our Courthouse."

Space limitation leaves the writer no choice but to leave untouched to future manuscripts the many towns, mining districts, areas (including Yosemite National Park), families, events, and more that played their equally important parts in what we continue to create today—our history.

For many centuries the Southern Miwok Indians inhabited, most peacefully, this western slope of the Sierra Nevada mountain range. They became a part of the balance of nature and lived very lightly on the land. Their philosophy was to leave the land at their passing as they had found it when they were born. Many of our problems on this earth today would not have materialized had we taken their ways rather than forcing ours on them.

Because of the abundance of these Native Americans in the great valley and its eastern slopes, early attempts by the Spanish explorers to establish settlements were not successful. Although a Spanish name and a Mexican land grant are about the only inheritance from the period of Hispanic possession, both have been of lasting significance.

The Spanish name, Mariposa, like so many others in California, will always be reminiscent of the first European culture to figure in the history of this colorful state. A foremost explorer, Alférez Gabriel

Moraga, and a little band of twenty-five buckskin-clad soldiers left the Mission San Juan Bautista and journeyed into the autumn heat of the Valle de los Tulares via Pacheco Pass and San Luis Creek. They crossed the San Joaquin River on September 27, 1806, and during the afternoon encountered great quantities of butterflies. The party camped that evening on a slough not far from the main river. Here diarist and chaplain of the expedition, Father Pedro Muñoz, made notes of the events of the day. "This place is called Las Mariposas (the butterflies) because of their abundance." Las Mariposas thereafter became associated with the stream that bears its name today.

We must skip through the next four decades of Mexican rule and state only that with the decline of the missions came the rise of the ranchos with their large acreage, indefinite boundaries and usufructuary titles. Seeking one of these ranchos because of his public service, erstwhile governor of California Juan Bautista Alvarado petitioned Governor Manuel Micheltorena, in a document dated February 23, 1844, wherein he asked for ten *sitios ganado mayor*, or ten square leagues of land. A patent was drawn up and signed by the governor on February 29, 1844 to a tract of land henceforth to be known by the name "Las Mariposas." This tract was located somewhere between the great valley of the San Joaquin, the Sierra Nevada mountains and the Chowchilla and Merced rivers.

Alvarado did not comply with a single requirement necessary for the perfection of his title. He never took possession of Las Mariposas or even visited it, because of difficulties caused by the political revolution led by Jose Castro, the Mexican War, and the ever-present Indian dominance of the area.[1]

With title based on the governor's signature, the conditions of the patent unfulfilled, and the grant still unlocated, Alvarado sold Las Mariposas to John Charles Fremont. The famous topographer, ex-

1. For those readers wishing a more complete record of proceedings of the involved legal history of the Las Mariposas land grant, one must look to the Expediente. This record of proceedings contains copies and original documents concerning the progress of Fremont's claim and may be found in the archives of the U.S. District Court in San Francisco. It covers the proceedings from February 23, 1844, until final confirmation to J. C. Fremont in 1855.

plorer, and agent for the promoters of Manifest Destiny entered the picture at this point. His influence on what later became Mariposa County was a major factor in the outcome of events told in this book.

Fremont, in his *Memoirs*, published in 1887, related the adventures of his third expedition west and the events that led to the Bear Flag Revolt and eventually future statehood. On December 18, 1845, while traveling southeasterly along the eastern slope of the central valley, intending to meet Joseph Walker and the remainder of his party as they traveled north, Fremont camped for the night on the south bank of the Merced River, which he called the Aux-um-ne. While continuing on the next day, the party came across a fresh trail leading into the hills of what Fremont called the "Horse Thief" Indians. The group of four whom Fremont sent ahead to reconnoiter soon were surrounded by warriors from the nearby village. Hearing shots, the main group hurried ahead and dispersed the attacking Indians. Being on good defendable ground, Fremont and his men camped for the night and left early the next morning to continue their journey south. Fremont recorded in his journal that they camped that night on a creek "with a slate bed." This leaves in dispute whether they were on Agua Fria Creek near the later town of Agua Fria or on Dead Man's Creek farther south in what is now called the White Rock area. Fremont's first adventure in the Mariposa region was an omen of the trouble he was to have there within a few years.

Failing to meet Walker in the upper reaches of the Kings River, Fremont returned to Sutter's Fort and then went on to the vicinity of San Jose, where he was joined, in the middle of February 1846, by the major branch of his expedition under Walker. This large group aroused the suspicion of the Mexican officials, and Fremont and his "topographical engineers" were ordered out of Mexico. He moved north to the shores of Klamath Lake, where he was overtaken in May by Lieutenant A. H. Gillespie with written and verbal orders from Washington.

Fremont immediately returned to the Sacramento Valley, where the presence of his force was sufficient to stimulate the formation of the California Republic, which was composed of American settlers who hoisted a flag showing a grizzly bear and a lone star. When war actually broke out in California on July 7, 1846, Fremont was on hand with his force and cooperated with U.S. Navy Commanders John D. Sloat and Robert F. Stockton in the conquest of California.

At the capitulation of Cahuenga in January 1847, Fremont accepted the Mexican surrender. Stockton appointed him governor of California, a position he held for two months until he was caught up in the quarrel between Stockton and General Stephen Watts Kearny. Kearny had been sent overland by orders from Washington and arrived in California late in the campaign. His orders conflicted with Stockton's, leaving Fremont caught in the middle. Fremont's decision to side with Stockton later was used against him during the court-martial brought by Kearny for insubordination.

In November of 1846, while governor of California, Fremont deposited with Thomas O. Larkin, U.S. Consul in Monterey, government drafts in the amount of $4,000 to buy a ranch for him. Larkin accepted an 18 percent discount and credited Fremont's account with $3,280.[2] About this time Alvarado and his wife offered Las Mariposas for sale at $3,000. Larkin, having power-of-attorney from Fremont, executed the transaction, passing title to Fremont on February 10, 1847. For this service, Larkin charged Fremont 7½ percent or $225 commission. The granting of this title was by no means perfect and would cause Fremont nearly endless trouble until 1855.

En route to Washington in Kearny's custody, Fremont, while camped on the Bear River in June of 1847, appointed Pierson B. Reading to act for him in developing a settlement on Las Mariposas. Joseph Willard Buzzell, a California pioneer of 1842, with money, equipment to build a house, cattle and horses, left for the Mariposas tract from the Cosumnes River with Reading's backing. The area to be settled was the Mariposa River near the foothills of the mountains. Because of his apprehension of the hostility of the Indians, Buzzell tried to set up farther down the creek but was driven away. Twice during the summer of 1848 he tried again, with the same result. It was a

2. All of the Larkin account books are in the Bancroft Library, University of California.

faltering beginning for a tract of land that would dominate the whole history of the Mariposa region to the present time.

Undoubtedly the greatest influence on the Mariposa region was the discovery of gold on January 24, 1848 in the mill race of James W. Marshall's saw mill on the American River, although its impact was not felt along the streams this far south until one year later.

At the time of the discovery of gold in California, Fremont's trial was ending with his being found guilty of mutinous and insubordinate conduct. President Polk remitted the judgment but Fremont's pride had been damaged and he resigned from the army.

Private capital raised in Saint Louis paid for Fremont's fourth expedition, to establish, it was hoped, a preliminary survey for a railroad by a southern route through the Rocky Mountains to the Pacific. After losing all his animals and about half of his personnel, eleven men, due to an extremely cold winter and poor judgment, Fremont continued west. Approaching the Colorado River, he met a party of Mexican miners from Sonora en route to California. While some writers say that Fremont heard for the first time of the discovery of gold the previous year from these Sonorans, the record indicates that he had been aware of the discovery while yet in the East.

While Fremont was making preparations for this fourth expedition to the West, another mission, composed of one man, headed east. Acting-Lieutenant Edward F. Beale, United States Navy, was about to play his part in the California gold rush. Commodore Jones needed an official courier to travel hastily to Washington, and Beale volunteered to go at his own expense. His orders were to proceed by the most expeditious route and deliver four dispatches to the Secretary of the Navy.

The intrepid sailor switched from quarterdeck to saddlehorn and made a historic ride across Mexico that would rank with that of Juan Flaco. But Beale's ride, unlike Flaco's, was an incredibly hair-raising experience in a savagely hostile country, at great risk to his life. From Vera Cruz he traveled by ship to Mobile, Alabama, then up the Mississippi and Ohio rivers to Pittsburgh, then by stage to Washington.

He arrived at the capital in mid-September 1848. The various dispatches from Commodore Jones, Consul Larkin and Minister Clifford and the samples of gold Beale brought with him were the first official news, the first hard evidence, of the great California discovery.

In February 1849, James Duff, soon to become a long-time resident of Mariposa, left Philadelphia by ship with a stamp mill, for crushing gold ore, ordered for the Las Mariposas by Fremont. It seems apparent that Fremont knew of the gold discovery before embarking on his ill-fated fourth expedition.

The record also shows that Fremont knew there was gold on the Las Mariposas. Dick Owens had shown him particles at the time of the encounter with the "Horse Thief" Indians. Either he dismissed the particles as iron pyrites, or more probably he didn't relish tarrying to look for gold with 200 hostile Indians making overtures to attack.

Before we get too far afield let us return to Fremont's meeting with the Sonoran miners at the Colorado River. An arrangement was made with the leader of the party for twenty-eight of the Mexicans to proceed to the Mariposas and mine the gold on a fifty-fifty basis. Alexander Godey, Fremont's next-in-command, would lead this group to the grant, and Fremont would go on to Monterey and San Francisco, where he was to meet his wife, Jessie.

After establishing a residence in one wing of the governor's house in Monterey, Fremont came up to the Mariposas in June or July 1849. Upon his arrival, he learned that the Sonorans, under the leadership of Godey, had found rich deposits of gold in quartz lying on the surface and were crushing this ore in arrastras. Having been gold miners in Mexico, they knew that the placer gold in the creeks had a source. This source or vein was found in the area of what later became the Mariposa Mine.

Of course news spread of these discoveries and within days the Mariposa country was deluged with gold seekers. During the autumn and winter these prospectors overran the stream beds, discovered rich districts and laid out camps, some of which became permanent settlements. Not only did miners rush in from the older districts to the north, but Mariposa, as the southern limit of the placer grounds, was the first mining area encountered by the overland emigrants who followed the southern trails into California. The Lone Star State was well represented. Texans, many of whom had been Texas Rangers and had seen service in the Mexican war, appeared in Mariposa early in the autumn. One of their number, Angevine Reynolds, and his partner, H. S. Richardson, told of digging out fifteen to twenty dollars a day from a small claim at the mouth of Chicken Gulch, using only knives and tin pans. Reynolds later was prominent in Mariposa history as an expressman, county clerk and newspaper editor.

The large population, soon at work both above and below Fremont's mine, gave rise to the town of Mariposa, which sprang up in October 1849 as the first settlement of any magnitude along Mariposa Creek. In the spring of 1850 high water washed out most of the buildings, or shelters, of the town, forcing the residents to a more favorable location on higher ground where the town now is laid out. Log Town, a smaller settlement, appeared at this same time about one-half mile upstream.

Also in the fall of 1849, the San Francisco banking firm of Palmer, Cook and Company took a lease from Fremont for permission to work a part of the vein near the Fremont mine. A small imported mill was set up on Mariposa Creek just south of the present townsite. It was probably the one James Duff brought from Philadelphia, leaving there in February 1849. The name was changed to the Mariposa Mining Company, and with added capital it became the first million dollar corporation in California.

The following spring (1850) the company sent a crew of fifty men to the Mariposa operation. Among them were storekeepers, mechanics, gamblers, miners, a restaurant man, and a surveyor, Mr. C. Armstrong. The flat above Mariposa Creek, 300 yards north of the Mariposa vein, was surveyed and laid out in streets. The main sixty-foot streets were named for members of the Fremont family: Charles, Fremont's middle name; Jessie, his wife; Bullion, Jessie's father's nickname; and Jones, for Wm. Carey Jones, married to Jessie's sister. The fifty-foot-wide cross streets were numbered, starting with First at the south near the mine, through Seventh at the north.

Before locating the rich Fremont or Mariposa vein, Godey and his

Sonoran miners had worked the placer gold with great success in Agua Fria Creek, westerly from Mariposa. Their places were immediately taken by some of the hordes of miners scrambling over the countryside looking for a place to stake a claim. At one location the creek bed was extremely wide and very rich. Here, in the summer of 1849, the town of Agua Fria, meaning cold water, sprang up. Called Agua Frio even on official state documents, it soon became the largest settlement in the southern mining region. Therefore, the newly-formed California legislature chose "Agua Frio" to be the county seat of the new Mariposa County.

The first election in California was held somewhere on the Merced River. On August 1, 1849, ninety-two men, appointed election officers, elected an alcalde, sheriff and other officials, and then they vanished. The men elected are not found again in Mariposa County records. The miners in Mariposa, as elsewhere for the first two years, lived under a system without civil law but with summary justice.

Delegates from ten districts met in Monterey in September 1849 and drafted a constitution patterned on that of Iowa. They then petitioned Congress for admittance to the Union as a free state.

Fremont was not a member of this constitutional convention but when the first legislature met in December 1849 he and Wm. M. Gwin were elected the first pair of California senators. George W. Wright, of Palmer, Cook and Co., and Edward Gilbert were the two representatives. Because of the slavery issue, it was almost a year later, on September 9, 1850, that California was admitted to the Union. During this wait the California legislature went on with its political organization.

The work of dividing the state into counties was delegated to a committee of which well-known Californians Mariano G. Vallejo and Pablo de la Guerra were prominent members. The committee's report, asking for the creation of twenty-seven counties, became law with the governor's signature on February 18, 1850. The picturesque nomenclature of the earlier Indian and Spanish was appropriately retained in all but two of the county names.

The counties smallest in size were formed of the greatest population, thus making Mariposa the largest of all in area. Management of so large an area—it covered one-fifth of the state—was a nearly impossible task, given the modes of transportation and lack of today's communications. Within a year the boundaries of Mariposa County began to change, and forty-three years later, all of Merced, Madera, Fresno, Kings, Tulare, Kern, and portions of Mono, Inyo, San Bernardino, Los Angeles, and San Benito counties had been formed. From these births, so to speak, Mariposa County has been christened "The Mother of Counties."

On March 2, 1850, the state legislature passed an act ordering an election of officers in each county on the first Monday of April. On Sunday, March 31, 1850, a caucus was held in Agua Frio [*sic*] to nominate candidates for the various Mariposa County offices. However, a ticket had not been formed by the next day, whereupon the meeting was continued in one of the drinking and gambling places.

Map of California showing original twenty-seven counties. Those with the largest population were the smallest in area.

Finally, on May 13 a panel of officers was chosen and the following men elected: judge, James M. Bondurant; sheriff, James Burney; clerk, Samuel A. Merritt; recorder, J. C. Bland; treasurer, Edward Beasley; district attorney, Orrin A. Munn; assessor, Thomas K. Munk; coroner, B. S. Scriven. Two justices of the peace and two constables were elected for each of the six districts in the county. The county judge and two justices of the peace composed the Court of Sessions, with powers both judicial and legislative.

James A. Bondurant, first county judge of Mariposa.

The promise of gold was often stronger than the lure of public position; therefore there were frequent changes in the first few years. The first meetings were held in the log and canvas house of Sheriff James Burney. More on the political aspect of this period will be found in following chapters.

The Native Americans in the Mariposa region were becoming increasingly resentful of the intrusions of the miners. Indian troubles culminated in the Mariposa Indian War and the white man's discovery of Yosemite Valley, 1851-52, events which make up a highly dramatic chapter in Mariposa County history and a chapter that has been told and retold only from an intruder's viewpoint.[3]

From 1850 Las Mariposas would dominate the historical development of the Mariposa region, as it would be a controlling factor for the next thirteen years in Fremont's life. It promised him wealth but it was to bring him unending trouble and disappointment. Because of Fremont's world-wide notability, it was fairly simple for him and his agents to enter into the era of big business. Soon seventeen joint stock

3. This part of history from the Native American's perspective awaits publication. Until then, if readers wish to become acquainted with this unpleasant episode, we might suggest they read Carl P. Russell's *One Hundred Years in Yosemite*; Lafayette H. Bunnell's *Discovery of Yosemite and the Indian War of 1851*; and Robert Eccleston's *The Mariposa Indian War 1850-1851*.

Now Know Ye. that the United States of America in Consideration of the premises, and pursuant to the provisions of the act of Congress aforesaid, of the 3rd March 1851. Have given and granted, and by these presents Do give and grant unto the Said John C. Fremont as aliente of Juan Bta. Alvarado, and to his heirs, the tract of land embraced and described in the foregoing Survey. - To have and To hold, the Said tract with the appurtenances, unto the Said John C. Fremont as aliente of the Said Juan Bta. Alvarado and to his heirs and assigns for ever

In testimony whereof I Franklin Pierce President of the United have caused these letters to be made Patent, and the seal of the General Land Office to be hereunto affixed.

Given under my hand at the City of Washington this Nineteenth day of February, in the Year of Our Lord one thousand eight hundred and fifty six, And of the Independence of the United States, the Eightieth.

Franklin Pierce

By the President

Jo. S. Wilson acting Recorder of the General Land Office ad interim

Recorded in California Record
General Land Office
Folio 1. Page 1. to 23 inclusive

Filed Monday March 28 1857 at 10 A.M and Recorded at the request of R.A. Lockwood Esq

R. S. Miller
Recorder of Mariposa County

Copy of last page of patent granting Fremont title to the Las Mariposas Estate and signed by President Franklin Pierce.

Map of Fremont's Las Mariposas Grant as re-surveyed in 1855 by order of U.S. Supreme Court.

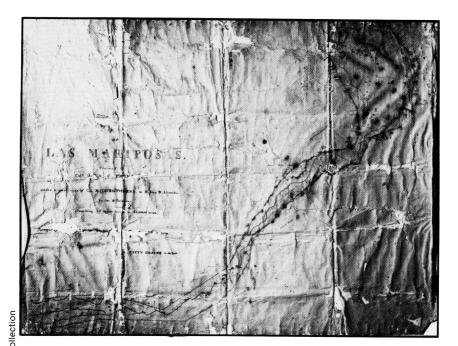

Original Las Mariposas Pan Handle map as surveyed by von Schmidt in 1852. Handle follows the length of Mariposa Creek. Pan encircles the towns of Mariposa, Mount Bullion, Agua Fria, Guadalupe and Bridgeport.

gold mining companies were on the market in Europe. Investment in these companies was anything but sound business practice, for the title to the Las Mariposas, like all the Spanish and Mexican land grants in California, had not yet been determined by the federal government.

Case number one on the docket of the U.S. Land Commission was the Las Mariposas. The law firm of Jones, Tompkins and Strode, augmented by Rufus A. Lockwood, provided an accurate knowledge of the legal procedure to follow. The commission ordered a survey of the grant, which was done, using a sketch map provided by Alvarado. This survey was made during the months of April and May 1852 by Allexey W. von Schmidt. The original of that map is in the possession of the California State Mineral Exhibit in Mariposa. There are, however, numerous copies of von Schmidt's notes. It will be sufficient to say here that the case went through appeals to the U.S. Supreme Court, which ruled Fremont's claim valid on March 19, 1855. The new ruling also ordered the said land to be surveyed in the form and divisions prescribed by law for surveys in California and in one entire tract. The survey was approved by the surveyor general on July 31, 1855. Patent to Las Mariposas was signed by President Pierce on February 19, 1856.

As the reader will find in later chapters, the signature of the president was not the end of Fremont's troubles with Las Mariposas.

Las Mariposas Estate as re-surveyed in 1855 describing Fremont's patent.

2 Courthouse Construction

As mentioned in Chapter 1, the town of Agua Fria was selected as the county seat of Mariposa County, and business was conducted from rented buildings. An entry in the Court of Sessions minutes of that time directs the county treasurer to pay Sheriff James Burney $165 for the use of his house for holding court, stationery, candles, etc.

While the county was suffering many inconveniences in administering the affairs of government in Agua Fria, the town of Mariposa was growing and prospering. A news account in the *San Francisco Daily Alta California* would inspire any prophet of the diggings to foresee that one day Mariposa would become the county seat. The prophet's prediction would soon become reality, as the state legislature passed an act on April 25, 1851 ordering the residents of Mariposa County to select a permanent county seat at the next general election, September 3, 1851.

Although the tally was not recorded, Mariposa must have received the most votes, because on October 13, 1851, the Court of Sessions minutes state: "Ordered by the Court that notices be posted in five public places that the County Seat will be in Mariposa from and after the 10th day of November next."

In Mariposa, county officers were again faced with having to rent space in which to conduct county business. The Court of Sessions now met in the home of Edward C. Bell, county clerk, which was at the southeast corner of Charles (Highway 140) and Sixth streets, and for which the county paid $100 a month rent. During the summer the great outdoors was the answer, according to "Blue Shirt," a Mariposa correspondent to the *San Joaquin Republican*, a Stockton newspaper. On June 14, 1852, he wrote that "a pleasant arbor . . . answers the triple purpose of church, courthouse and town hall."

Suitable space in which to conduct county business would have to

Woodcut of the town of Agua Fria, first county seat, before it was destroyed by fire in 1866.

wait, as it appeared the need for a jail would take preference. Sheriff Burney provided space for a jail in Agua Fria, which meant that prisoners had to be transported to Mariposa and returned at the expense of the county.

On April 10, 1852, the Court of Sessions awarded a contract to Pendleton Hill for the construction of a new jail for the amount of $3,835. This two-story log structure was built near the middle of the block formed by Charles Street (Highway 140), Mariposa Creek, Fourth Street and Fifth Street. At the June 16 meeting of the court they approved the addition of an eight-foot-wide porch in front of the upper story, to be supported by four columns, and also the construction of a trap door and a door in the lower partition. For these additions Hill would be paid $700. The logs were cut by Tom Early in Logtown, about one mile north.

On April 7, three days before the contract was awarded for the jail, the grand jury recommended the construction of a courthouse. We must point out that because of the fluid movement of the miners, taxes were hard to collect. Also, most of the buildings were tents or rock and logs, hence no tax base on improvements. It was doubtful the county could pay in full for the jail, so on June 7, 1852, during its construction, the Court of Sessions set a tax rate of twenty-five cents per $100 assessed valuation for "the erection of Public Buildings." It was another two years before the topic of a courthouse appeared in Court of Sessions minutes.

The year 1854 would see many improvements in the county and the town of Mariposa. One of the first of these was the establishment of a newspaper. On January 20, 1854, the first issue of the *Mariposa Chronicle* was published. A year and a half later, under new owner-ship, the name was changed to the *Mariposa Gazette*. In the February 3 issue of the *Chronicle*, the editor brought attention to the need for a place to conduct the county business. He pointed out that one was needed not only for the convenience of the public, but also as a matter of economy, as $300 a month was going for rent. He wrote a colorful description of the meeting space endured by the grand jury, saying that the trial juries were being compelled to reach "sage conclusions," the foreman either on a rock or stump and the jurors gathered around him, as old Virgil says, "under the patulous shade of an umbrageous fig tree."

Either in the due course of events or because of prodding by the press, on April 21, 1854, the Court of Sessions discussed erecting a courthouse at Mariposa, and on the following day discussed plans and financing. The plan submitted by Perrin V. Fox was adopted on June 21, and on July 21, 1854, a contract was awarded to Perrin V. Fox and Augustus F. Shriver in the amount of $9,000 to construct a 40½-foot by 50½-foot two-story courthouse. The building was to be completed by January 1, 1855. The site, "on a high eminence," was donated to the county by William R. Owen. We must point out to the reader that ownership of Fremont's Las Mariposas Grant would not be settled for another year. Therefore, Owen only had "squatter's rights" and could not deed the land. On September 5, 1860, for the sum of one dollar,

Fremont deeded to the county the town block for the courthouse.

Skilled craftsmanship is what one should think of when admiring the

Perrin V. Fox in later life after returning to New England.
George Towne Collection

Mariposa County Courthouse. On August 14, 1854, the Court of Sessions accepted the bond of Fox and Shriver and, presumably, work commenced. It was the age of hand-planed boards, square nails, wooden pegs and pioneer resourcefulness. Everyday goods and materials were shipped to San Francisco and then to Stockton, from where they were freighted by wagon to Mariposa. Fox and Shriver found this system to be impractical and chose to build this classic edifice from native materials.

As to who supplied the lumber, it is not clear. We find reference that it was cut from a fine stand of "White Pine" less than a mile from the courthouse. That would be Logtown, behind the present public cemetery and where, in 1852, Humphrey and Geiger had a hand-forged vertical-blade saw mill powered by an overshot waterwheel. In the history of the David Clark family, the claim is made that Clark cut the lumber for the courthouse at his steam-powered vertical-blade mill on Bear Creek. This mill was near the intersection of Highway 140 and Triangle Road where the original Clark house still stands. Both locations could have been used, given the length of time in which the building had to be constructed and the fact that the production of these mills was less than 5,000 board feet per day. Whatever its source, the lumber was delivered and apparently on time.

We find that Fox and Shriver also used native materials in the form of a slate rock foundation. Upon this they laid an eight- by eight-inch wood plate on which the building would stand. Also a slate foundation and wooden plate were placed under the two walls running the length of the center hall. The supporting "balloon style" framework was strengthened by mortise and tenon cuts at the points of contact. For

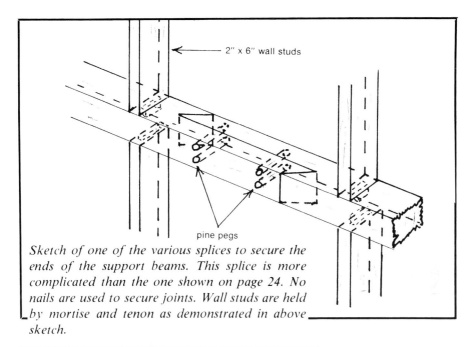

2" x 6" wall studs

pine pegs

Sketch of one of the various splices to secure the ends of the support beams. This splice is more complicated than the one shown on page 24. No nails are used to secure joints. Wall studs are held by mortise and tenon as demonstrated in above sketch.

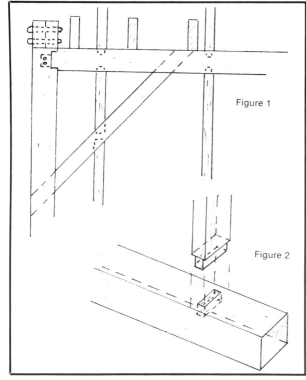

Figure 1

Figure 2

Sketch of support structure showing mortise and tenon and wooden pegs at joints.

Figure 1 is a typical corner at ceiling level of first floor and support beams of second floor.

Figure 2 demonstrates how tenon protruding from vertical timber fits into support beam.

those not familiar with the terms, to mortise means to notch in, and the tenon is a projecting piece designed to fit into the mortise.

Ponderosa and sugar pine were used throughout the building, including doors. There were no nails used in the supporting framework. The joints and splices were secured with pine pegs. Square nails were used, however, to fasten the floor, wall and ceiling boards to the framework. The lumber came to the job site just as the saw blade cut it. There were no planing mills, so the smooth surface and the tongue and groove edge were made with the carpenter's plane. When we look at the walls, floors, ceilings, and outside siding, it is difficult to comprehend that all that surface was smoothed by hand. The marks of these craftsmen are still evident even on the spectators' benches and the nine-foot judges' stand. It wasn't until the 1968 restoration project that the sawdust and shavings were removed from where they had fallen under

Original floor plan. First floor.　　　　*Original floor plan. Second floor.*

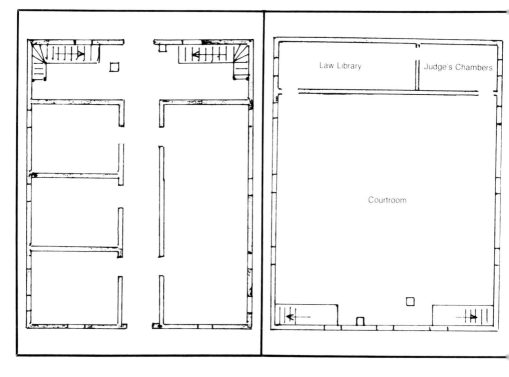

the building 114 years before. When completed, there were four offices downstairs and the courtroom, law library and judges' chambers upstairs.

The contractors completed their project on time, as recorded in the Court of Sessions minutes at its first meeting in 1855, on February 12. The court also accepted the building, with minor additions which brought the total building costs to $9,200. The $200 over-run is not bad by today's standards.

The building of the courthouse was attracting attention elsewhere. On November 3, 1854, the *San Joaquin Republican* reported that the building was about completed and sat on a "high eminence which overlooks the city, and gives a fine view of the surrounding country." However, the merchants of the town were not impressed with this view. They wanted the building to be moved closer to town. This idea did have some merit, as the town, as originally laid out, stopped at Seventh Street.

At one of the first hearings in the new courtroom, an enterprising lawyer moved to have the case dismissed on the grounds the courthouse was outside the town of Mariposa and therefore not in the county seat. Before his case could be heard, a chain of events occurred, beginning with a law passed by the state legislature that all counties were to be governed by a board of supervisors. Until then, the Court of Sessions had acted in a judicial and also a governing capacity in Mariposa County. A special election was held on April 9, 1855, at which time three supervisors were elected, each representing one of the three districts of the county. All were elected on the popular plank that the courthouse be left where it was, and they backed this up at their meeting on May 14, 1855. They accepted the courthouse, ratified all prior actions of the Court of Sessions, and adopted a new town map. Upon examination of this map, we notice that the streets now extended to Thirteenth, thus placing the courthouse within the town. A very subtle way of solving a sticky problem. When the lawyer's case came to trial, his motion was denied.

Paying for the building was not solved so easily. At this same May 14 meeting, the supervisors authorized the county treasurer to pay to Fox and Shriver what funds were in the public building fund at that time and also to draw a warrant in Fox and Shriver's favor whenever that fund exceeded $300. Payments continued until the end of 1858. Fox and Shriver took the county to court on July 23, 1859 for final payment of interest owed.

Additions to the courthouse have been numerous, and on the remaining pages of this chapter we will discuss them briefly. The first was a brick vault with three-foot-thick walls in which to safely store the county records. A. F. Shriver, again, submitted the low bid in the amount of $2,500. It was accepted by the supervisors on March 1, 1861. Lest the reader is wondering about Mr. Fox, he had returned to New England before the suit with the county.

The vault was added to the north side of the building adjacent to the county clerk's office. We noticed that Shriver's bond was double the amount of the bid. Perhaps the supervisors were still smarting from the lawsuit. We needn't remind the reader that it wasn't Shriver that defaulted on his bid.

The only deletion to the building of any consequence, other than changing interior walls, was the removal of one of the front staircases

From inside 1861 vault looking into county clerk's office. Original local-fired brick wall around doorway. One-inch thick plasterboard placed over interior walls and ceiling in November 1965 to protect the deteriorating brick.
Leroy Radanovich Collection

Courthouse after 1884 picket fence and before 1891 vault. County officials: No. 1, Fred Schlageter; No. 2, William Turner; No. 3, Joseph Ridgway; No. 4, Ed Skelton; No. 5, Judge Corcoran; No. 6, Judge L. F. Jones; No. 7, Samuel Counts; No. 8, George Temple; No. 9, Gus Robinson; No. 10, Maurice Newman; No. 11, James H. Lawrence; No. 12, Newman Jones; No. 13, Henry Farnsworth.

leading to the courtroom. This will be discussed in more detail in a later chapter. We will say here that on November 7, 1863, the board ordered "that the vacant room known as the Treasurer's Room be enlarged so as to take in the stairway to the courtroom above, and the window." This meant that the right hand hall wall would be extended to the front wall as it is today. The stairway remained in this room, which in later years was used as the district attorney's office, until 1947, when it was finally removed upon request of the newly appointed district attorney, Robert Curran.

The cupola and clock were added to the courthouse in 1866; however, the reader will have to wait for the explanation until the chapter devoted entirely to this controversial addition is reached. With all the agitation over the clock, the building of a chimney slipped in almost unnoticed. On May 8, 1866, Charles S. Peck's bid of $226 was approved for a chimney with a fireplace in the clerk's office. All we know of the fireplace is that it shows in the picture taken inside the clerk's office sometime in the 1890s and that it had been boarded up before it caught fire in 1903. The stovepipes from all the downstairs offices were connected to this chimney. The falling soot caught fire but was quickly put out with a couple of buckets of water after the wood covering was removed from the opening. The stoves were removed in 1960, and in December 1974 the chimney was placed forever out of use when it was filled with concrete and steel, with the blessing of the personnel in the clerk's office. It seems the sounds they had heard coming from the covered fireplace were created by a family of owls— "whoooo" were removed before the chimney was filled.

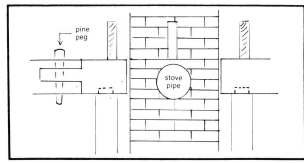

Sketch of 1866 chimney in clerk's office, with wall boards removed, showing splice held with pine peg in main beam supporting second floor.

Following the events of 1866, the next twenty-five years would pass with no additions to the courthouse, principally because this was a time of decline in the county. Mines were operating spasmodically and the population had declined. Not unlike today, paper continued to accumulate in county government, to the point that the small vault was overflowing. On July 10, 1891, a year after rejecting the first bids, the supervisors awarded a bid to build another vault to Charles S. Peck. His bid was $1,800. The new vault, also constructed of brick, would be added to the 1861 vault.

On November 28, 1891, the editor of the *Gazette* had this to say: "To most of us, it would appear that the addition to the courthouse vault is assuming gigantic proportions, in regards to additional expense and extra time, but we presume there is some valid reason for the extra Two hundred and fifty dollars and lengthened time." As in

County clerk's office about 1890. Door to vault left center, fireplace lower right. Left to right: R. B. Stolder, district attorney; Samuel Counts, treasurer; Fred Schlageter, deputy sheriff; George Temple, justice of the peace; John M. Corcoran, superior court judge; sitting in glare of window, Mollie Egonhoff, superintendent of schools; also sitting, Joseph Sterne, deputy assessor; Morris Newman, county clerk. Courtesy of Mariposa Museum and History Center

the case of the clock, the vault was accepted when completed. On December 19 the editor concluded with: "The Hall of Records is at last completed, as far as the contractor's part is concerned, and presents quite a handsome and creditable appearance. It is large enough to supply all needed room for records. Its walls are cemented and the floor is laid in fine concrete blocks, and after all the grumbling all of us have done, we are really proud of it." Because of the bars on the windows, visitors frequently still mistake the building for a jail.

Here we must consider the fence that surrounds the square. Periodically, during the first decade after the courthouse was built, the supervisors would come under fire for allowing "innumerable hogs to nest under its stately walls" by not fencing the courthouse square. Finally the supervisors called for bids after the newspaper had stated

Courthouse before 1926 metal fence and after columns and front door trim were painted to resemble granite in 1909. Note addition of 1891 vault.

that a "niggardly economy was causing this public property to become a barnyard and a hogpen." On February 12, 1866, bids were opened and A. F. Shriver's was accepted. However, Shriver declined to enter into a contract unless he was paid in cash. County scrip was worth seventy-eight cents on the dollar and he didn't want to get caught on the short end again. It was ordered that the matter of the fence be postponed for an indefinite period of time. The "indefinite period" came to an end eighteen years later, on July 7, 1884. The bid to construct a picket fence around the courthouse square was awarded to A. W. Josselyn when the amount of $725 was approved. The picket fence was replaced by the present wire fence on March 1, 1926. It was still needed to restrain the stray donkeys, cows and, yes, the occasional hog, that continued to roam the town.

The courthouse received one of the first six telephones installed in Mariposa. On November 4, 1895, the supervisors ordered that a telephone be installed in the clerk's office and that seventy dollars worth of coupons, to be used exclusively for county business, be purchased from the Sun Set Telephone Company.

Beginning at the end of 1899, certain offices were lit with Criterian acetylene gas (carbide system). On October 25, 1907, the gas lights were replaced with electric lights. The board ordered that lights be installed in the clerk's office, the vaults and the jail. A hydroelectric generating plant had been built on the Merced River, at Bagby, by the Mariposa Commercial and Mining Company, which had run a transmission line to power its mines at Bear Valley, Mount Bullion and Mariposa.

By the end of the 1890s, the economy of the county had picked up. The mines were beginning to open, logging was becoming an industry, and there was talk of a railroad's being built to Yosemite. This building boom and population increase were felt in the crowded offices of the

Courthouse in 1960s. Note Native Daughters Cedar Tree planted in 1930 and blown over in 1988. Metal fence replaced pickets in 1926. Rowney photo, Mariposa Museum and History Center

MARIPOSA COURT HOUSE

Courthouse and 1900 annex before 1926 metal fence. Note foundation is painted to look like brick. Also wooden front steps. Metal benches are the same ones on the grounds today.

courthouse. More space was needed. The supervisors responded by having L. B. Chenowith, of Bear Valley, add a four-office annex, separated by a thirteen-foot breezeway, to the rear of the courthouse on July 5, 1900. This cost the county $1,500 and subjected the board to criticism by the grand jury for not following the bidding procedure.

From its first coat of paint to the present, the courthouse exterior has been all white in color except for one time. The one exception was in February 1909, when the board of supervisors hired W. A. Scott at the rate of four dollars per day. Supervisor Stolder was appointed to oversee the project. At this time the columns at the corners were painted to resemble granite blocks. We don't know if this was Stolder's idea or Scott's, but it must not have been acceptable to the populace as within a few years the columns were white again. The reader will hear more about Scott in Chapter 6.

Again there was a slump in the economy because of the closing of

Courthouse after W. A. Scott painted, in 1909, the corner columns and front door trim to resemble granite blocks. The clocktower was also trimmed in a darker color. This must not have been popular with the citizens as a few years later the pictures show the courthouse all white again. The gentlemen are unidentified.

mines and a drop in the population. Hiring a janitor in January and calling for bids in July for fuel to heat the offices in winter were the highlights of the next thirty or more years. Mariposa County never felt the depression of the '30s as severely as did most of the nation. With the price of gold rising in the 1930s, the front pages of both the *Mariposa Gazette* and the new paper, the *Mariposa Miner*, were filled with news of more mines opening up. State Highway 140 had been extended to Yosemite National Park and Highway 49 from Sonora to Mariposa. The S.E.R.A., the N.R.A., the W.P.A. and the C.C.C. were providing

1935 addition during construction. Second story built on top of 1900 annex and breezeway between main building and annex enclosed. Small windows mark restrooms.

public works projects that brought workers into the county. One of these projects was an extensive addition to the rear of the courthouse. Not all approved of it, most notably John Dexter, the editor of the *Gazette.*

On the front page of the February 28, 1935 issue, Dexter took the officials to task in a long article titled "All Californians Would Oppose Remodeling of Historic Courthouse," a classic article that is still timely. With the placing of the monument in front of the courthouse by the Native Sons of the Golden West in 1929, the building was on its way to becoming known for its historical importance. Dexter was one of the first to draw attention to this. Economics must have overruled historical significance as the project did continue. All agreed that more space was needed for county offices; the disagreement was where it would be provided. The issue of altering the courthouse to provide space for expanding county needs surfaced again in future years, and the idea was consistently rejected by citizens dedicated to protecting the integrity of the famous old structure.

Thus, the last major structural changes to the building, completed in 1935, included doubling the length of the courthouse by the addition of a second story onto the 1900 annex, enclosing the breezeway, moving the restrooms inside and putting the stairway in the main hall.

The *Gazette* editor kept his readers informed on the progress being made, and upon completion of the project had this to say: "Certainly the builders of the Mariposa Courthouse did honest work and used honest materials, as was shown during the recent reconstruction work, which required the exposure of the inner framework and construction done by the '49'rs. The old courthouse certainly is a monument to the faithfulness, integrity, and honor of those pioneers who 'Builded Well.'"

Before public sentiment against destroying the integrity of the historic courthouse became dominant, one last addition was slipped in. This was a small projection from the north wall of the auditor-recorder's office which is now included in the clerk's office. The supervisors awarded the bid for this work to C. C. Bettencourt in the amount of $1,285 on May 27, 1948.

Of course, following all of the additions, more furniture was needed. In an attempt to return to the early appearance of the interior, a request went out in 1957 to all those counties severed from the "Mother County," Mariposa, for surplus furniture. All eleven responded with gifts including chairs, desks, and even chandeliers. These may be seen throughout the building today.

The need for serious restoration was recognized in about 1960 because of the sway developing in the roof and the tipping of the cupola. An engineering firm was engaged to produce a structural and safety report. The strengthening of the 1861 vault roof began a series of projects designed to reinforce the building and lengthen its usable life. The cupola, roof trusses, south wall, front wall, front stairway to the courtroom, and the 1891 vault were all restored by 1973. The following year the building was further protected by the installation of a Life Safety System (interior sprinklers).

Proposed museum and library addition promoted during 1954 Centennial. Never accepted after strong opposition by those dedicated to preserving the integrity of the courthouse.

The 1987 restoration project became a reality because of the State of California Parks and Facilities Bond Act of 1984. Two separate applications led to the approval of $150,000, and the county appropriated another $40,000 for matching funds, contigencies and architect's fees. Most of the county's allocation came from the Courthouse Restoration Fund set up in 1983 to receive donations and certain court fines.

We cannot provide space here for even a brief synopsis of the work that almost completed the restoration of the original structure, but we can give the reader an idea of its magnitude. Mariposa County Contract No. 87-7 was awarded to David Wise, Natural Environments, in the amount of $136,000, to remove the interior wallboards and floor in the clerk's office; excavate under the building; remove the boards from the interior north wall of the courtroom; update all electrical wiring; install insulation in walls and attic; place one-half-inch plywood on interior walls for strength; strengthen roof trusses; replace all original boards removed during the project to their exact places; paint in the original 1854 color all surfaces disturbed during the work. In the course of the project, another $21,000 was required for change orders, mostly to correct hidden structural damage.

As the reader has most likely surmised, there was a logistics problem to be solved. The solution was that the entire county clerk's office—staff, files and furniture—was relocated in the basement of the Hall of Records, across the street from the courthouse, during the six months of work. Superior Court was held in the Arts and Crafts Building at the fairgrounds, three miles away.

We must praise County Clerk Gerald McCarthy and staff for their cooperation, and also the public for putting up with the inconvenience. The architect engaged by the county since 1978 to oversee the courthouse work is Robert McCabe, a respected restoration architect in Sacramento. The daily documentation of work done and historical information uncovered during the project was made by the author of this text.

As this book is being printed, yet another restoration project has been funded and will go to bid. Mariposa County Parks and Recreation Director Richard Begley, who successfully submitted the application for the 1987 project, has obtained a grant from the 1988 State Proposition 70 in the amount of $253,000. It is expected these funds will nearly complete the restoration of the entire courthouse.

3

Cupola and Clock

As we said earlier, "The Clock" deserves a chapter all its own, due to the controversy and popularity it has attracted since its inception. The decision of the supervisors to have a cupola built on the courthouse to house a clock was not exactly popular. Many of the citizens felt a fence should have first priority on any funds spent.

The editor of the *Mariposa Gazette*, A. M. Swaney, took up the issue with these sarcastic comments: "It is expected that the people will be able to distinguish the exact time for a mile, that the bell attached will be heard easily all over the county and part of Frezno [*sic*]. Courts will be run by it, and jurymen and witnesses in default, punished for delay, and even the executioner will swing off the unfortunate condemned as the clock, by its strike, gives forth the hour. It would well be a very extra affair, the courthouse ain't fenced in and how unfortunate if some of the scores of hogs that have their nests around there, should poke their nose under the corners and shake the pendulum off of time."

We should mention here that A. F. Shriver, who had not come to terms with the county over his cash-only bid on a fence, did not give up. His low bid on May 9, 1866 for erecting the cupola was in the amount of $275.

Now we turn our attention again to the *Gazette* as the editor continued his vendetta on the clock and its sponsors. In the May 19 issue is the comment: "Clock not up yet. When will the Board build a town pump?" In the next week's issue: "Clock not been put up." On July 7: "That clock on the courthouse is sure to be a fixed fact, the framework has been mostly put up, and gives an indication of how it

Facing page: Courthouse "on a high eminence" before clock. 1860 Carleton Watkins salt print.

Clock and cupola added in 1866.   Leroy Radanovich photo

will look when finished. The clock is reported on the way here and it is supposed that before many more days elapse the good people of town will be informed of the hour of the day and night by this new improvement, as bell is attached which is expected to strike the changes in reliable order." [4]

By now editor Swaney was referring to the clock as "that clock." July 28: "That clock is at the courthouse and two men of skill have been trying to get it together for several days. It is the 'Elephant' of the Supervisors." August 18: "That clock is being put in order." And then on August 25: "'That Clock' on the courthouse is up and running. And the hours are pounded out as they pass the heavy bell that beats with a

4. There are no marks on the works of the clock, but on the bell is the following: Naylor Vickers & Co., 1861—Shefield.

regularity quite unexpected. The cost of the things has been considerable, and it required much labor to put it in order, but it is humming away now and is really quite an improvement to the place." (It was the next day, August 26, 1866, that a fire destroyed the major part of Mariposa's business district, between Fifth and Seventh streets—over sixty buildings. The fire started in the office of the *Free Press*.)

It would appear that editor Swaney had resigned himself to go along with the times, to use a play on words, and call off his attack on the clock. This would not be the last of his attraction to this timepiece, as we will see later. The bill to the county from McDermott & Co., a local business, is quite interesting, and we take the liberty to copy below from the original bill of sale:

McDermott & Co.
Mariposa, California
August 14, 1866

1 clock and dials	$720.00
Drayage in San Francisco	1.50
Steamboat freight	6.50
1765 lbs. freight	26.47
1 cast steel bell, N2399 weighing 267 lbs. at 45¢	120.15
Yoke and standards	20.00
Steamboat charges on bell and dials	3.50
Drayage in S.F. bell & dials	2.50
Paid freight on 860 lbs.	12.90
For extra freight and insurance on dials, $2.00 each	8.00
Delivering dials and bell	2.50
Delivering clock	2.50
	$934.68
Commissions, including exchange on San Francisco Co., 5%	46.73
	$981.41
Agt. 1, Lumber, Clock	2.00
	$983.41
Scrip at 87¢	$1130.35

The reader will notice that the last item refers to county scrip, which was worth eighty-seven cents on the dollar.

James G. Bell had a local watch and clock repair business. He put the

Bell showing Sheffield, England 1861 casting date at the top. This was an adapted church bell. The wheel for a rope and the clapper are not used as the clock works strikes the bell with a mallet. Weight of bell is 267 pounds.
Leroy Radanovich photo

clock together and billed the county $128 for sixteen days' labor. On September 3 he sent the supervisors the following proposal:

> To the Honorable Board of Supervisors of Mariposa County,
> Gentlemen:
> I herewith present to you my report on the clock:
> The time part will run for one week.
> The running or striking part, 60 hours.
> I propose to you to keep the clock in good order with accurate time, oiling, winding up and repairing same, for the term of one year (1 year) with the exception if some large cog wheel should break, for which I shall not be liable, for the sum of One Hundred and Eighty Dollars ($180.00) in funds of the county.
> All of which I respectfully present
> Yours,
> James G. Bell

Nothing is recorded in the board minutes; however, it is assumed that they accepted Mr. Bell's proposal to keep the clock wound. The county had not yet begun the practice of hiring a janitor for the courthouse. At this time the insurance was raised to $10,000 on the building to include the cupola and bell.

The good behavior of the clock ended in a few years, however. On April 1, 1870, the editor of the *Gazette* had this to report: "The weights of the town clock, weighing nearly 1,000 lbs., fell last week from the

Clock works. Note the two drums upon which the cables are wound to run the timing and the striking. Also the clock face that matches the ones on the cupola. Leroy Radanovich photo

belfrey to the ground, passing through three floors of the courthouse as if no obstacle were in the way. Luckily no one happened to be underneath, although people were passing and repassing very near the line of descent of the ponderous weights. Mr. Thomas thinks that as the clock is constructed, it will be nearly or quite impossible to prevent this thing from happening occasionally, without impairing the usefulness of the clock."

One would get the impression from the article that the weights went crashing through the floors, breaking wood. This could not be the case, as the cables on which the weights are hung descend almost to the ground as the clock unwinds. Therefore, a boxed well would have been built when the clock was installed.

Two of these wells are in place and used today. The one visible to the public is against the front wall, on the inside and to the left of the left door as you enter. The other may be seen in the courtroom near the right aisle. The weights on this cable fell in the early 1980s, almost hitting Supervisor Beverly Barrick while she was at her desk. The protective boxed well had been removed temporarily while the room was being renovated. These weights are stacked on the cable like the weights on a platform scale and could fall off if the cable were wound with a jerking motion, or as in this last instance, when they caught on the ceiling.

Making the clock a topic of comment has continued as editors of the *Gazette* changed. James H. Lawrence was the editor in September 1876 when this comment was made: "'Slow and sure' is the motto of the town clock, when it starts to strike the hour you may be sure it will get through the task in the course of human events, but there is no guarantee that you live to see it a fact accomplished. The other day when a stranger came to town soon after noon, he inquired whose funeral was going on. We explained that it was only the town clock announcing the dinner hour, and then he wanted to know whether it was finishing up from the day before or just commencing for the next day."

As editors change so do custodians of the clock. Surveyor R. B. Thomas replaced James Bell in February 1870 and was paid twenty-five dollars per month to keep it running and in repair. Four years later his salary was reduced to fifteen dollars per month, not as a result of his poor performance, but as a result of less money in the county coffers due to the slipping of the local enomony.

Another change was made in March 1884, when the supervisors appointed Thomas McElligott to take charge of the courthouse clock at ten dollars per month. They also hired him to repair defects in the clock tower in December 1887, after the grand jury paid it a visit. A prior grand jury hadn't been so favorable. In February 1879 it recommended to the supervisors that they "expend no further on the courthouse clock, as we deem all such expense a waste of money and entirely unnecessary. In our judgement the money necessary to keep said clock running may be used for better purpose." They felt a new carpet in the courtroom was more justified.

The job of special custodian ended in December 1894, when Joseph C. Lind was appointed janitor at the courthouse at a salary of twenty dollars per month. We might assume that he would keep the clock wound—but not forever, as "he" became a "she" when Mrs. C. Schwing was appointed janitor in January 1914, at thirty-five dollars per month. Possibly she had difficulty turning the crank that wound the heavy weights; at any rate, in December 1915 Patrick H. McElligott was allowed the sum of six dollars per month for the care of the courthouse clock. Pat was the brother of Thomas, the former custodian. The two of them came to the Mariposa area in 1875. Now enters the second generation of keepers of the clock with the appointment of James P. McElligott, the son of Pat, in January 1920, at a monthly compensation of six dollars.

More pressing news now requires our attention. "Vandals Wreck Hands of Mariposa's Famous Clock" was the headline on the front page of the April 4, 1930 issue of the *Mariposa Gazette*. Editor John Dexter continues: "Quick action and clever detective work on the part of Sheriff Castagnetto, Undersheriff Ellingham and Deputy Earl "Bub" Johnstone resulted in bringing to justice one of the members of a party who broke and tore away the hands from the historical old clock, on the courthouse at Mariposa on the night of March 31. It may have been April Fool's Day for the rest of the world, but to the residents of Mariposa it was vandalism on the part of those who tore away those ancient hands and disfigured the historical timepiece that has withstood the ravages of time and been protected with tenderest of care by all for sixty-five years."

The mood of the citizens had been darkening ever since the early morning discovery of the missing hands. Because of this, Justice of the Peace W. A. Scott decided to hear the case at his residence instead of open court. This decision would cost him the next election. Editor Dexter echoed the frustrations of the people. In the next issue he wrote: "To most of the people of Mariposa, it appears that injury was heaped upon insult as a result of the manner in which the recent trial was handled in the local Justice Court. The great injustice done the public was the 'Star Chamber' methods adopted by the Justice in conducting the case."

Dexter goes on to say that the offender "was never compelled to appear before the public and be subjected to the gaze of the people he insulted; rather than this, he made a number of private trips to the abode of the Justice and there it is said upon one of these trips he paid a fine of one hundred fifty dollars, while the public waited at the courthouse to hear the pleadings of the prisoner and the reprimands that should have been offered by the Justice for the crime committed." The culprit was a member of a group of U.C. Berkeley students on their way to Yosemite. This is the only vandal damage the courthouse has had of any consequence up to this date.

A brother of James, Maynard McElligott, used his "reconstructive powers" and repaired the hands so that they could be used again.

We cannot leave this chapter without reference to the one last time the clock "kicked up its heels." Editor Dexter had some fun in his January 31, 1935 issue with the following: "The clock in the courthouse tower went on a strike—or rather, a striking spree—Sunday morning, and the way the old girl struck was a caution. Most people thought she was suffering from a stitch in her side, while strangers in our midst thought that the incessant strikes were the tolling of a bell in respect to the memory of a departed one of prominence and venerable years. At 9 o'clock she cut loose of 27 strikes, or strokes, but that was only a mild beginning. At 10 o'clock she developed some real speed and turned loose for 98 consecutive strokes. But not until 11 o'clock did she show just what she could do. At that hour she ticked off a total of 156 strikes. This brought her to within one of matching her own previous record, established some ten or a dozen years ago, when she turned loose 157 strikes in succession. Some seemed to feel that the striking spree might mark the end of the old girl's long years of service. But they guessed wrong, for she is still on the job dishing out the time with reasonable accuracy, and striking the hours correctly."

As she continues to do.

Aerial picture of the courthouse taken in 1932 from a Jenny airplane.
Courtesy of John Fulham.

Merced Motorcycle Club field day, outing and race in 1918.

Welcome ceremony after 1926 and before the placing of the monument in 1929.

4   Celebrations

The courthouse with its surrounding square has played host to most of the large gatherings of note during our county history. An opportunity for a gathering to commemorate the laying of a cornerstone was evidently missed when construction of the courthouse began. There is no record of its being laid nor is there a record of a dedication ceremony when the building was completed. The need for a building in which to hold meetings of culture, theatricals, concerts and balls was met with the construction of the Opera House in the late 1850s. This was replaced by the Concert Hall, which in 1917 was followed by the Liberty Hall, the new Masonic Temple.

We would not attempt to give the reader, even if we knew, a chronological list of all the miscellaneous uses the courthouse has endured. We will attempt to make a statement that will point out its multiple contribution to its citizens. One cannot depend entirely on the board of supervisors minutes for all the information needed to give us an insight as to how the courthouse was used other than for official business. From the newspapers we find, mainly, the more notable functions. One would need to have access to and research the minutes of all the organizations, churches and lodges to come close to having a clear picture of the building's "other life."

From today's perspective, it's hard to imagine that all the county departments were housed under the same roof of this 40½- by 50½-foot building. We do know that at times the homes and businesses of an elected official were used as office space. Since this was a decision made for his own convenience, the county paid no rent. We also know that spaces were rented for some offices. The offices of sheriff, treasurer, coroner, surveyor and superintendent of schools, depending on the elected official, were at times elsewhere. The clerk, auditor-recorder and assessor appear to be the ones firmly entrenched in the courthouse itself, probably because of the need to safely store the county's official records.

The separation of church and state was brushed aside when, on occasion, a traveling minister would use the courtroom for services. Fraternal organizations used the facilities for a period of time until more suitable quarters could be found, especially after the two disastrous fires in the town. Christmas parties, including a tree with lighted candles, were referred to on more than one occasion. The fear of fire must not have been as prevalent then as today. That fear has led to a ban on smoking anywhere in the courthouse.

The area in front of the building proved to be a favorite place to congregate for group pictures of county officials and for departures and homecomings. One picture, taken between 1926 and 1929, shows a group, mostly women, in front of the courthouse, which has been decorated to "Welcome" a group yet to be identified.

The courthouse was a few months less than seventy-five years old before the first celebration of any significance was held there, and then it was not to honor the building. The occasion was the unveiling and acceptance of the quartz monument with a bronze plaque that still holds a position of honor. It has appeared in all the pictures taken thereafter of the front of the courthouse. This monument was erected by the Native Sons of the Golden West after permission was granted by the supervisors, on April 1, 1929.

Newspaper accounts written after the April 21 event gave a glowing report of over five hundred people taking part in and witnessing the event. It seems a good-sized delegation from Mariposa met the Merced caravan at the historic old Millerton Road. This was on Highway 140 at the Merced-Mariposa county line. A brief stop was made to welcome the Merced delegation to Mariposa, during which time Miss Merced, Bernadine Maddux, and Miss Mariposa, Katherine Dexter, daughter of the *Gazette* editor, exchanged greetings and baskets of flowers. The combined caravan then proceeded to the courthouse via Bridgeport, Buckeye and Mormon Bar.

An appropriate program at the monument followed, arranged by the Yosemite Parlor, No. 24, Native Sons, of Merced. The dedication

Dedication on April 21, 1929, of quartz monument and bronze plaque in honor of pioneers of Mariposa County by Yosemite Parlor No. 24, Native Sons, of Merced. Superior Court Judge J. J. Trabucco delivering brief summary of the early history of the courthouse.

ceremonies consisted of a group of Boy Scouts raising the American flag on the courthouse flagstaff, followed by Miss Merced and Miss Mariposa unveiling the monument on behalf of the Native Daughters of the Golden West. The plaque, dedicated to the pioneers of Mariposa County, was presented by P. R. Murray, president of Yosemite Parlor, and the acceptance speech was made by Superior Court Judge J. J. Trabucco, who "in his masterful way" gave a brief summary of the early history of the county and the historical courthouse. His acceptance was followed by words from May S. Givens, grand trustee of the Native Daughters, who introduced Grand President Dr. Louise Heilbron. National Park Director Horace M. Albright, H. R. McNoble, Joseph Barcroft and others rounded off the ceremony. A basket lunch was enjoyed in the courthouse square, following which the caravan returned to the San Joaquin Valley via Bear Valley, Quartzburg and Hornitos.

We find reference that the square granite base of the monument came from the Mount Ophir Mine, where it was used during the early days in an arrastra, and the quartz rock and crystals for the pyramid-shaped monument were gathered from the famous mines throughout the county. Recently a motion picture film made during the affair has come to light and has been transferred to video by Leroy Radanovich. A sound track will be added once those on the film have been identified. To our knowledge, this is the first moving picture of the courthouse.

We could have devoted this entire chapter to one celebration because of its sheer magnitude involving practically the whole state over its ten-day duration. If the reader desires a more detailed description of all that went on, he or she must turn to the many newspaper accounts, especially those in the *Mariposa Gazette* and the *Merced Sun Star*, that were written prior to, during, and immediately following the event. I am sure that many of you know by now that I am referring to the centennial celebration of the courthouse and the *Mariposa Gazette*. Any oversight of these "pride and joys" of the county on prior milestones in their history was made up for during this celebration.

The honor that this event brought to the county would not have

Centennial of courthouse and Mariposa Gazette. *Governor Goodwin Knight on left shaking hands with general chairman, Superior Court Judge Thomas Coakley. E. Clampus Vitus members looking on.* Rowney photo

come about if it had not been for the herculean efforts of one man, Judge Thomas A. Coakley. Not only was he a superior court judge, but as the county would soon find out, he was also a promoter. This county was not a stranger to hosting events that brought people from near and far, such as the 49'er Fiesta Days, the Labor Day county fairs and the Givens Grove barbecues. The centennial event was planned to surpass them all.

True to the spirit of all successful events staged here, the Centennial was planned and produced by volunteers. A committee was formed in 1953, with Judge Coakley as overall chairman, and the groundwork was laid. At the start, financing was, of course, a major issue. For this

Centennial of courthouse and Mariposa Gazette. *"Chief" Lee-mee, Chris Brown, demonstrating Indian dances.*   Rowney photo

county to shoulder the financial burden could be compared to an ant carrying an elephant. Therefore, the judge called on individuals, commercial interests and the state bar association for help, and from their response the financial goals set by the Centennial Committee were met.

Because the courthouse is the seat of government for all of Mariposa County, the Centennial Committee made sure all of the county would be involved in some way. The dates chosen, May 7-16, 1954, would present the county at its finest, weather-wise, with natural wildflowers, green hillsides and water in the creeks. The residents would respond by shutting down everything except those services essential to the celebration. Most were involved in some way in conducting the myriad of events.

The daily program for all included tours of historical places, wildflower excursions, golf, fishing, demonstrations, Indian dancing and gold panning, to name just a few. No corner of the county would be forgotten, from Wawona golf, Yosemite Valley group meetings, Greeley Hill School concerts, to Hornitos historical tours—all contributed their part. The crowds of spectators did their part by swelling the population of the county by over five thousand during each of the ten days.

There also were special events to be attended on most of the ten days. On the second day the courthouse was honored by a special ceremony which was followed by the first of seven deep-pit barbecues at the fairgrounds. This same pit would be used to cook the meat for all dinners, leaving little time to burn more wood for coals on which to bury the next load of meat.

On this same day was the large "Parade of the Fifties" from the courthouse to Highway 140 and the lower end of town. A few days later another large "Parade of the Fifties" was followed by ceremonies conducted at the courthouse by the State Bar of California commemorating the 100th anniversary of California's oldest courthouse. The crowning glory bestowed on the courthouse was the ceremony at which State Supreme Court Chief Justice Hugh Gibson proclaimed the courthouse "A Shrine To Justice In California." Another distinction was the calling of the calendar of the state supreme court in the courtroom. It was the first time in the history of the state that this honorable body had met officially out of its chambers.

On the last day of festivities, May 16, the special events included an Oldtimers' Reunion in the courtroom. Later that afternoon the culminating ceremony was a marking ceremony at Agua Fria, the first county seat. I cannot begin to convey to the reader the exhilaration felt by the whole county in playing host to the thousands who attended the celebration. Even though exhausted, most were sorry to see it end and were confident it would be another 100 years before it could be topped.

The next ceremony did not directly involve the courthouse; however, that building's prestige was borrowed upon on March 22, 1968, to help launch from its front steps and lawn the fund drive to build a combined history center and county library. Again, Judge Coakley

Fund raising ceremony on March 22, 1968, to launch the construction of a new library-museum. School children sent "up and away" balloons to mark the event. Rowney photo

would preside as general chairman and, with his exceptional leadership and ability to engender enthusiasm amongst the citizenry, the financial goals were exceeded and the new building was dedicated on May 23, 1971. By now, the courthouse was gaining a reputation of being the place from which to launch a successful enterprise.

The courthouse contributed its share to the festivities in conjunction with the 1976 celebration commemorating the two hundredth anniversary of the United States of America by being accepted as a national historical landmark. Harry Stewart, a member of the county's Historical Sites Commission, successfully submitted the application after two previous attempts by others had gone awry.

Fund raising ceremony on March 22, 1968 to launch the construction of a new library-museum. Gold nugget award winners holding plaques, left to right: Francis Appling, Kay Varney, Bret Bagwell. Standing behind: Historical Society President Bob Hill. Seated: author, Shirley Sargent.
Rowney photo

Events connected with the nationwide celebration were scheduled in the county throughout the year. However, those involving the courthouse were planned for the Fourth of July weekend. The gala commenced on Friday, the second, with the Maid of Mariposa Pageant at the fairgrounds. On Saturday, the formal dedication of the 122-year-old courthouse as California Historical Landmark No. 670 began at 2:00 p.m. The address was made by then-Assemblyman Ken Maddy, later to become a state senator. This was followed by a large parade through the town of Mariposa, a deep-pit barbecue, and a dance that continued into the early hours of the morning.

Twenty-five years after the centennial observance, most residents were ready to attempt another celebration. This was planned for June 8-10, 1979, and of course included the *Mariposa Gazette*. The courthouse again was the center of activities.

"Heritage of Law and Press 1854-1979" was the fitting theme chose. On Friday, the Fifth Court of Appeals led off the weekend by holding three hearings in the courtroom. Mariposa County's former state senator, George Zenovich, returned as a member of the court. In the afternoon, the courtroom was the scene of a mock trial conducted by the San Joaquin College of Law, a reenactment of a murder trial held in the same room in the 1850s. Jesus Torres was tried and sentenced one day and hanged the next.

The following day, Saturday, the wagon train that had started from Wawona the previous morning arrived in Mariposa at noon. It then became part of a large parade through town. After the parade a dedication ceremony was held at the old 1858 stone jail by the Matuca Chapter, E. Clampus Vitus. A plaque was affixed to the building at this time. The day was topped off with a deep-pit barbecue at the fairgrounds (these barbecues have now become a tradition in Mariposa).

Sunday started with an old fashioned camp meeting sponsored by the combined Mariposa and Cathey's Valley Methodist churches and

Ribbon cutting at front door of courthouse during re-dedication ceremonies on May 11, 1988. Left to right: Gerald McCarthy, county clerk; Eric Erickson, chairman, board of supervisors; Leo McCarthy, lieutenant governor; George Towne, great grandson of courthouse designer and builder, Perrin V. Fox.
Leroy Radanovich photo

held at the same place as those in the late 1800s. At a meeting of the Mariposa County Historical Society, the history and virtues of the 125-year-old courthouse were outlined in a speech by Noel C. Stevenson of the Yuba-Sutter Bar. Throughout the weekend, tours for the public were conducted at the courthouse, jail and the downtown I.O.O.F. Hall. All agreed they had witnessed a fitting tribute to the two old enduring institutions.

The last celebration involving the courthouse, up to this printing, took place on May 11, 1988, when the building was rededicated following the completion of the $190,000 restoration project. Perhaps dedication should be the term, as there is no record of one being held upon the building's completion in December of 1854. Also at this time was the official swearing-in of the recently-appointed sixth superior court judge of Mariposa County, Richard McMechan.

These May 11 ceremonies were held on the lawn in front of the courthouse. Lt. Gov. Leo McCarthy was the featured speaker and also administered the ceremonial oath of office to Judge McMechan. McCarthy told the crowd of about two hundred fifty people that the ceremony was not just the rededication of the courthouse but "it rather was the rededication of a symbol which stands for the rule of law in Mariposa County and for the tenacity of the people of the county." A special guest was George Towne, the great-grandson of the building's designer, Perrin V. Fox. A catered no-host luncheon was served on the lawn following the program. All agreed that it was a fitting ceremony even though there was no deep-pit barbecue and it was 134 years late.

1987-88 courthouse restoration project personnel: left to right: Todd Barnes, associate engineer, county public works department; David Wise, Natural Environments, contractor; Robert McCabe, architect; Scott Pinkerton, courthouse historian, author; Richard Begley, county parks and recreation director; Gene Itogawa, program administrator, State Office of Historical Preservation; Mike Morata, State Historical Sites Commission. Picture taken by co-author Leroy Radanovich. Leroy Radanovich photo

5

Strange and Humorous

While researching the material for this book, I realized that one chapter must be devoted to some incidents that have made past newspaper editors and other writers wax whimsical. Also, for a building of the stature of our courthouse, it has had more than its share of strange occurrences, not only within its walls but also to its inhabitants.

The first was probably the incident involving the county treasurer, J. .F. A. Marr, in December 1851.

Anyone who has read books written about lost treasures, or is aware of early Mariposa history, has heard the tale of the lost fifty-dollar gold coins. One wonders how many thousands of tons or yards of creek beds have been turned over by treasure hunters looking in vain for the subjects of this myth. We will not waste space here repeating all the fantasy that has persisted over the years, but will provide the reader with the facts, which are just as entertaining. This will dispel once and for all the sham that has been perpetrated on the unsuspecting.

One of Mr. Marr's duties, as Mariposa County treasurer, in 1851, was to collect taxes on licenses granted by the Court of Sessions on commercial enterprises such as saloons, ferries and toll roads. It seems that he was lax in his duties. The Court of Sessions minutes for December 5, 1851, contain a grand jury report that instructs the treasurer to comply with the law and make his collections, which appear to be incomplete, and also recommended that the district attorney have the law enforced against all persons violating it. The report was signed by Charles D. Simpson, foreman of the grand jury. On December 11 the committee appointed by the grand jury to examine Mr. Marr's books found that the examination was premature and they were discharged. It appears that Mr. Marr was, at that time, in the act of complying with the grand jury order and was out and about the county doing just that.

We will depart from the facts at this point to give the reader an insight into the tale as it was told. Mr. Marr had made his collections and upon returning to the county seat was drowned while crossing a stream on horseback. Both he and his horse were lost, along with a reported $15,000 in fifty-dollar hexagon gold coins. Now in reality, this amount was in excess of all the taxes collected in one year in the county. The "hexagon coins" referred to were, in truth, the octagon-sided fifty-dollar gold coins circulated under permit from the United States government by the private Moffat Mint in San Francisco. Another myth is that they were struck in a "mint" at Mount Ophir. However, that is another story and has nothing to do with this book and the courthouse. As the reader can imagine, these coins—and a few do exist in private collections—would be worth far more than their face value today, thus the attraction to locating where they were believed to have been lost.

Any student of early Mariposa County history knew that this tale could not be true because even in those days, and especially after the grand jury investigation, the loss of public funds would have to be accounted for. There was nothing in any of the records to support such a story.

What was lacking over the years was documentation as to what happened. This came to us in the following letter, of which we have a copy, and was the basis of an article written by this author and published in the Spring 1981 issue of the *Sentinel*, the Mariposa Museum and History Center quarterly. The following letter was written in the town of Mariposa and dated December 30, 1851:

Dr Sir

Knowing that Mr. Marr, our worthy County Treasurer, addressed you a short time since on the subject of making his returns, I now write you to inform you that he is no more, consequently some further delay in the premises will be unavoidable. However, the Court of Sessions have this day appointed his successor, who will immediately enter upon the discharge of his duties, and will make his returns at an early day.

The circumstances connected with his death are melancholy indeed. Upon addressing the letter to you, he immediately set out for the San Joaquin,[5] a very remote section of our county, where he collected some seven or eight hundred dollars, and on his return he came to the crossing of the Mariposa some eight miles from this [place] where he was found, supposed to be drowned, but a jury of inquest declared that he had been murdered, which was strongly corroborated by three distinct compressed fractures of the skull, evidently the effects of blows inflicted by a cushioned London billy or sling shot. Since which, however, his pantaloons containing the money have been found, which, were it not for the evident marks of violence on his head, would fully corroborate the first impression that he was drowned.

I am Your Obedient Servant, Edwd C. Bell, Clerk

The handwriting of this letter was compared by this author with Mr. Bell's handwritten minutes of the Court of Sessions, and it is the same. As the reader has noted from the above, the money Mr. Marr had collected was recovered. As a result, like most treasure tales, this one had no basis in fact.

Now let us turn to a "lighter subject," the clock. The decision to place this in the Humorous Chapter will be obvious. We direct your attention, again, to the feisty *Gazette* editor, Swaney, and his next episode with the clock. November 10, 1866 finds him writing the following, about the bell's continuing to ring after striking the hour: "The town clock for the last week has had a violent attack of the 'Diaree' caused by a pro-lapsus of the spinal cord leading from the striking apparatus to the fallopian tubes, producing general derangement in the intestinal organs. Dr. Bell [the custodian] took his sexton and discovered a diagnosis about the diaphragm of the thing, and gave it Wrights, Brandeth's, Ayers, Cook's and Etyl's pills, which caused an earthquake in the abdominal regions of the regulator, placing the system in a healthy condition, from which, it is hoped it will never get out of order."

5. The "San Joaquin" referred to in Mr. Bell's letter was in the area of Fort Miller and Millerton on the San Joaquin River where there was a small village. Marr could have ridden horseback as far as Four Corners in what was soon to become Tulare County. At this time Mariposa County extended to Fort Tejon on the south and to the summit of the coast range on the west.

Evidently Mr. Bell was a good mechanic, or doctor, as indicated above, because in December editor Swaney followed with: "The clock. This valuable institution has maintained very good behavior lately, and such exemplary conduct deserves a passing notice. Stick to it, old fellow, we shall never begrudge you a good word as long as you are true to time." "Old fellow" must have behaved well enough to escape the notice of the press for the next ten years.

Bureaucracy in government has not changed. On April 3, 1890 the *Gazette* ran an article that reported that the county had purchased a new safe for the treasurer. On arrival, it was found to be too large to fit in the fireproof vault at the courthouse, so was put in Zeller's new store, downstairs under the Odd Fellows Hall, where it still resides. One wonders if the treasurer conducted business from the store at the time or if the money was transported the four blocks from the courthouse for safe keeping. Also, on what date did the county cease using the safe?

Some readers have heard the tale of the secret stairway in the courthouse. This is another of those untrue legends that has survived the years. Prisoners were reported to have been spirited out of the building and away from angry mobs by using these stairs. This was the way Deputy Sheriff Punch Choisser was supposed to have escaped a lynch mob with his prisoner, Indian Willie. Untrue, according to the record. When pictures of the front of the courthouse taken before 1947 are examined, we see that there were two stairways to the courtroom from the front of the building. The framework of the two can be seen crossing diagonally the upper corners of the downstairs front windows. Research has revealed that the stairway to the right of the front door was sealed off in 1863 by extending the hallway wall to the front of the building. Later the original wall was removed, making the district attorney's office larger and incorporating the stairs. Superior Court Judge J. J. Trabucco suspected that attorneys were quietly slipping up these stairs and unlawfully listening to the deliberations of the jury. His suspicions must have been well founded as he had the stairs sealed at the courtroom floor level where the patch may be seen today.

Over the years, reports of a ghost in the courthouse have been whispered. County Clerk W. E. Gallison and *Mariposa Gazette* editor John Dexter would tell the curious how they could on occasion hear

Front of courthouse showing the two stairways crossing at angles behind windows.

music coming from the large pot-bellied stove in the clerk's office. We do not know if both men were teetotalers or if others confirmed their claims. The same stove has had a place of prominence in the courthouse exhibit at the Mariposa Museum and History Center since 1972 and to our knowledge has remained silent; possibly it misses encouragement from its old friends.

Some of the wags of the courthouse would have visitors pause and listen for the tread of the resident ghost who would make the building creak just before the clock struck. This author has noted that the ghost must have started losing weight about the time the last building stabilization project was in progress, as the sound has become fainter. Now we tell the sightseers that the reason there hasn't been a fire of consequence since the courthouse was built is that the ghost doesn't want to lose his happy home. After finding burned insulation on electrical wires and direct shorting of metal conduit that could spell the demise of any other building, we trust the apparition will remain.

The editor of the *Gazette* took pride in pointing out to his readers, on

May 12, 1866, that the county business was being administered by a solid board. Of the three-member board of supervisors, Hendricks, the chairman, and McElroy weighed 200 pounds each, and McKinney weighed 246: a total of 646 pounds. He asks if any of our neighboring counties can beat that? Not too many years ago a member of our five-member board was heard making the claim that he was the biggest

Captain William James Howard, "The Mysterious Sheriff," on his ninety-seventh birthday.

supervisor in California. This left those within hearing distance wondering if he was referring to stature or political prominence.

The status of reverence gained early on by the courthouse has spared it from random vandalism over the years, except for the clock. There was one incident that went beyond this. A rash of break-ins involving the burglarizing of safes had been plaguing authorities in Mariposa and adjoining counties. During the night of June 14, 1966, entry into the courthouse was gained through a window in the assessor's office. The thieves entered Tax Collector John Mentzer's office through the pay window. They pried the door off the one-hundred-year-old safe, netting the thieves $42.50 which was Mentzer's personal money. No public funds were lost. To our knowledge this was the only burglary involving the courthouse since its opening. The steel cage around the pay window and counter that provided security between the public and the cash drawer in the tax collector's office was removed in 1971 when these offices became the present supervisors' meeting room. A section of this barrier has been preserved and presently is on display on the west wall of the county clerk's office.

Recently, while searching through back issues of newspapers, I was intrigued by this article: "Box of Bones Found in Vault of Courthouse. The charred remains of human bones have been found that were left over from evidence of a case 12 years ago when French Louie disappeared from his place and a man named Savage and his wife who lived at the same place were brought to trial." The law requires that evidence be kept for a specified number of years before it may be destroyed; then a judge makes the final determination. It was during this process that the bones were discovered. The above article appeared in 1901, so with the subtraction of twelve years, or "about," it brought to memory the story of the "Mysterious Sheriff" and how he solved a murder case from the experience of a vivid dream. The sheriff was Wm. J. Howard, then deputy sheriff of Township No. 4, the murdered man was Louie Herbert, and the accused were Peter Savageau and his wife, Thelma. The year was 1886.

The main character in this story is William James Howard. To prepare the reader for what is to follow, we give you this short resumé: Howard came to Mariposa County, as a grown boy, from Texas with some of the first forty-niners. His brother, Tom, followed later. After having some luck at mining, Howard established a 350-acre ranch in the Buckeye area, near Bridgeport. He named it Upper Buena Vista and sold supplies, purchased in Stockton, to the miners around the Mariposa area. Early in the 1850s, he and his brother, Tom, purchased another piece of property along the Stockton-Fort Miller Road, west of Indian Gulch.

The governor of California appointed Howard to be one of the California Rangers, a group of twenty men under the command of Captain Harry Love who were credited with the capture and death of Joaquin Murietta. In 1857, he represented Mariposa in the state assembly and later was a deputy sheriff. He married Isabelle Holton in July 1857, and the family resided at the upper ranch. In 1874 he built a house on the edge of Mirror Lake in Yosemite Valley, where the family spent the next ten summers.

Our "mysterious" story begins with the appearance in the town of Mariposa, in 1886, of a beautiful, exquisitely dressed Frenchwoman who introduced herself as Mrs. Thelma Savageau. She soon purchased a small cottage in town and furnished it in good taste. Louie Herbert had recently bought a small ranch near the Howard place where he raised vegetables, grapes and chickens. He made his living selling the produce to the merchants in town. While on one of these trips to the Bogan & Co. store, he chanced to meet Mrs. Savageau. As he was in great need of feminine companionship, the meeting soon blossomed into infatuation. He asked her to take care of him in exchange for a home, which she would inherit, along with the property, upon his death. Thelma agreed and a contract was drawn up by District Attorney Newman Jones, who was shrewd enough to put in the term "during my natural life."

About a month later, a young well-built man appeared in town, from the Mono mining area, claiming to be Thelma's husband, Peter. He was searching for a job in the Mariposa area. Soon he had moved in with the pair and everything appeared to be harmonious.

It was said that on more than one occasion Louie imbibed in old barleycorn. It was at one of these times that Howard saw him in Princeton and said, "You had better watch out or Savageau will find you this way and kill you." Louie patted his pocket, indicating he carried a gun and was not afraid.

Later that day, after a long horseback ride, Howard returned home and, being tired, lay down to rest for about an hour before the evening meal. While in a deep sleep he had a dream so vivid that it appeared he was a witness to a real murder. At dinner he told his family that they would not see Louie alive again. This alarmed the family and they wanted to know the details of the dream.

Some people are born with what is called a "sixth sense," and Howard, better known then as "Captain Howard," was one of them. So sure was he of what he had "seen" that he told his family that he had seen Louie come out of his barn and go to the house. Peter Savageau was waiting for him inside and hit him alongside the head with a two by four, killing him. Thelma Savageau was in the house and witnessed the murder. Savageau carried the body outside to a vineyard where he put it on the ground. He built a large fire and after it had burned down, creating a hot bed of coals, he threw the body on, along with more wood.

The next morning the vision of the captain's dream was as strong as the evening before. As he passed the Herbert place on his ride to the courthouse at Mariposa, he noticed that Savageau was riding Louie's favorite "Jack." Upon questioning, Savageau said that he was looking for his own horse who had run off. On arrival at his office, Howard related his dream to Judge Corcoran, District Attorney Newman Jones and Sheriff Mullery, who laughed when he said, "You'll never see Louie alive again."

No one saw Louie over the next few days, and when the Savageaus came into town and began loading Thelma's furniture into a wagon, the officers became suspicious. Knowing they would be thus engaged for a time, the captain took the opportunity to test his dream and rode quickly to Louie's place. Finding him gone, he went to the spot in the vineyard where in his dream he had seen Savageau burn the body. Scratching through the ashes, he found some charred bones, which he placed in a box. Upon returning to Mariposa he showed the contents of the box to Doctors Kearney and Turner. When they identified them as the bones of a human, a warrant was issued for the arrest of Savageau and his wife.

The next morning Howard and Sheriff Mullery left to arrest the Savageaus at the Louie Herbert place (in the vicinity of the present Frank Long ranch). They were taken into custody without resistance and brought to Mariposa. Savageau was placed in jail and his wife taken to the hospital for safekeeping.

At the jail, the captain gained the confidence of Peter Savageau and

Courtroom in the late 1960s before a modesty panel was ordered placed in front of witness chair in front of the judge's bench. Leroy Radanovich photo.

told him that he had found some of Louie's bones. Savageau exclaimed, "How could you?" Then the captain related what he had "seen." Savageau said, "Surely that was the way it happened and the captain must have been watching the whole thing," whereupon the captain said, "No, it was just a dream." Savageau made a full confession of the crime which Howard recorded in his notebook.

The people felt sorry for Savageau, who had exonerated his wife, because they felt sure that she had forced him to kill Louie Herbert. The trial took place in superior court on February 25, 1887. On March 4, 1887 the jury foreman read the following verdict: "We the Jury find the defendent Peter Savageau guilty of murder in the first degree and fix penalty as imprisonment in the State prison for life. Aug. Olny, Foreman." Thelma was found not guilty the same day.

The reader may still be skeptical, but the fact remains, Louie Herbert was murdered on December 4, 1886, the same day and hour that Captain William J. Howard had his dream.

6

The Courtroom

Little did P. V. Fox and A. F. Shriver know while they were building the courthouse that the judge's bench in the courtroom would become a sounding board for justice in California. In later years the main reason the courthouse qualified as a national historical landmark was because of the early precedent-setting cases that had been heard there.

In designing the courthouse Fox used the same Grecian architectural style that he had used in New England. The plain lines of the exterior were repeated on the inside. This is especially evident in the courtroom, where the wide hand-planed boards on the walls, the high ceiling, the straight-backed spectators' benches and simple furniture remain. The marks of the carpenter's plane and the judge's gavel are plainly visible on the bench that accommodated three judges during the Court of Sessions.

In appearance, the courtroom remains the same today as when it was built in 1854, except for the graining. Readers not familiar with the term "graining" are entitled to an explanation. It was the practice of the times, when the look of oak was desired, to paint that distinctive wood grain on the surface. To make the finished product look realistic took great skill and artistic talent which only a limited number of painters were able to achieve.

W. A. Scott, the judge in the clock incident of the 1930s and also a painter, was called upon to demonstrate his ability. During the month of March 1912, he fulfilled his bid of $320 to the county by wallpapering the downstairs offices and painting the upstairs. This included the graining of the furniture in the courtroom except for the modesty panel in front of the witness chair, which was not part of the original furnishings. The reader might be interested to know why that panel is there. By law, the witness must be seated in such a manner that his or her face may be seen by the entire jury. In this courtroom the chair is

*Courtroom show-
ing "graining" on
backs of spectators'
benches, painted in
1912 by W. A.
Scott.*

placed in front of, and to one side of, the judge's bench and in full view
of the jury. During the time that mini-skirts were in fashion, there were
those who frowned on wearing underclothing. Now the reader is ahead
of me. Needless to say, the presiding judge soon ordered a modesty
panel be installed. It was replaced during the 1977-78 restoration with
one that matched the lines of the bench. The painter on that project,
a local man named Ron Bown, added his touch with great skill by
graining each face of the panel in a different style of oak. The graining
done by Scott to the other courtroom furnishings in 1912 still remains.

Let us now turn to the judge's bench and point out its nine-foot
length. This was to accommodate the three judges that presided over
the Court of Sessions, the ranking county judge in the middle flanked
on each side by an associate judge who was a justice of the peace. As we
mentioned earlier, this astute body governed the county and also sat in
judgment of lower court cases until 1855, when a board of supervisors

Courtroom in 1933. The judge's bench is original and is nine feet long to accommodate the three judges that presided at the Court of Sessions. The county judge sat in the middle, flanked on each side by an associate judge.

took over the governing duties of the county. Mariposa County was included in the higher Thirteenth Judicial District, beginning in 1850 with Charles M. Creaner, followed in 1856 by Ethelbert Burke. This system of justice prevailed until the new state constitution was adopted in 1879 and the court system was changed to the one we know today.

There is only one superior court in California. When a judge is appointed to fill an unexpired term or is elected by his or her constituents, he or she is then a judge of the Superior Court of California. A superior court judge may be assigned by the California Judicial Council to hear a case in any jurisdiction in the state. Through the years, the low local case load has allowed Mariposa superior court judges to hear cases throughout the state, many of them precedent-setting.

The long bench in the courtroom was full again when the Fifth Court of Appeals met in the courtroom on June 8, 1979, during the three-day 125th anniversary celebration of the courthouse and the *Mariposa*

J. J. Trabucco, second superior court judge, at the bench in the same chair used today. Note "graining" of table and bench, done in 1912 by W. A. Scott.

Gazette. We might point out here an item of singular distinction to add to the laurels of the courthouse. It is a fact that all judges serving the county since the completion of this building have presided from this bench.

A question often asked by those touring this famed courtroom and, to our knowledge, unanswered, is why the two sets of seating to the sides of the judge's bench? We know that both were built during the original construction. One theory is that the witnesses called would sit in the benches to the right and the jury in the chairs to the left, thereby separated from the spectators. Sooner or later someone with a knowledge of jurisprudence will have a logical answer.

Superior Court Judge J. J. Trabucco had a fine reputation as a jurist. The record indicates that in all his thirty-five years on the bench he did not have a decision overturned. In an earlier chapter we made reference to Judge Trabucco's suspicions that some lawyers were in the habit of unlawfully listening, at the head of the stairs, to the jury's deliberations. This was possible because most of the time there was not an empty room in the building for them to use as a jury room. When the case was given to the jury, they stayed in place and the courtroom was cleared until their decision was reached. Frequently, this is the case even today.

One wonders, as laws change, how much longer the integrity and

John M. Corcoran
1st Superior Court Judge
1880-1903

Joseph J. Trabucco
2nd Superior Court Judge
1903-1938

Andrew Robert Schottky
3rd Superior Court Judge
1938-1953

Thomas J. Coakley
4th Superior Court Judge
1953-1969

Dean C. Lauritzen
5th Superior Court Judge
1969-1987

Richard L. McMeechan
6th Superior Court Judge
1987-

simplicity of this historic courtroom will be maintained. To protect this integrity, an open display of television cameras and computers must not be allowed.

As this is being written, there is the possiblity that another credit will be added to the fame of the courthouse and its courtroom. We mention it here because at this time the claim has not been disputed. A few years

Cartoon from San Francisco Chronicle *about J. J. Trabucco, second superior court judge, and his reputation of never having a decision overturned by a higher court.* Courtesy Mariposa Museum and History Center

ago a gentleman spent time at the courthouse researching a case that had been tried in the court some years back in which forensic evidence was admitted into testimony. He was quite sure that this was the first time forensic evidence was used in court in the United States. He had been researching the subject for some time and found that this case predated all earlier discoveries. He left in an elated frame of mind.

Law and order had been pretty well established in Mariposa County and somewhat throughout the state by the time the courthouse was built. To give the reader a glimpse of earlier attempts at law and order, we refer to the case of "The People vs. Jose Maria Hernandes." Theft had become so prevalent and intolerable by 1851 that the state legislature provided that in a case of grand theft, capital punishment could be imposed. In a case of petty theft, the defendant, if found guilty, could be flogged, not to exceed fifty lashes on the bare back, or punished by a combination of imprisonment, a fine, and lashes. In "The People vs. Jose Maria Hernandes," brought before the Court of Sessions, Hernandes was found guilty of petty larceny by the jury. His sentence was "that the prisoner be taken and given 50 lashes upon the bare back." Such a sentence had a two-fold purpose: the guilty was punished, and no jail space was required.

Before long this law would be repealed, as we find in the board of supervisors minutes of February 23, 1866. A claim was filed by Peter Lynch, in the amount of twenty-five dollars, for "Whipping D. McCaffrey as per special contract with the Board of Supervisors." District Attorney John M. Corcoran, later to become county judge and then the first superior court judge, must have advised the board on the change, as on the back of the claim is endorsed a rejection with the chairman's signature and the comment: "Just Bill but not Legal."

The advancement of human rights was still in its infancy and, in fact, the slavery issue would hold up the acceptance of California as a state for a period of months. What was commonplace in the youth of the courthouse would be shocking today. The people who felt oppression the most, during the gold rush in California, were the Native Americans. In the minutes of a board of supervisors' meeting on February 13, 1866, a bill from Dr. Grandvionet for holding an inquest on the body of a murdered Indian was rejected with the following comment: "Inquest on dead injun not considered a person according to law." By as late as 1879, in a trial before the district court, the perpetrators were found not guilty because the only witnesses, Indians, were not allowed to testify against them. They were still not considered human beings by law at that time (but they could testify against another Indian).

Peter Lynch's bill to the
county for flogging, rejected
by chairman of the board of
supervisors with comment:
"Just Bill but not Legal."
Filed February 13, 1866, by
A. Reynolds, county clerk.

Not all were equal in the eyes of the law in the late 1800s.
Thirteenth District Judge E. Burke's instructions to the ju

Laws did change in favor of the Indian, as we find in the divorce trial of John and Lucy Hite. John Hite arrived in the Mariposa area in the mid-1850s and mined Mariposa Creek, in the Mormon Bar area, with less than moderate success. He and about half a dozen others in the area were quick to leave these claims when there was news of a promising strike in the Marble Springs area, northeast of what is now Greeley Hill. The group was caught in a heavy snowstorm and two died, either from the cold or from starvation. When John again became aware of his surroundings, he was in the care of Maresa, an Indian woman, who brought him back to health. Later she led him to the gold-bearing ledge that became the famous "Hite Mine" on the South Fork of the Merced River.

With his good management, this mine made John a millionaire and a respected citizen of the county. Shortly after he started developing the mine, in 1862, Maresa died and John took up with Lucy, her sister. Lucy had previously lived with a man named Jerry Gibbs, long enough to bear him a son named Tom. John married Lucy, Indian style, and they lived together for twenty-five years. Lucy was a gracious hostess to the never-ending parade of guests and frequent opulent balls at the mine.

After John sold the mine he began to travel the west investing in all types of mining stock. Before his travels he built Lucy a comfortable two-story home in the Indian Peak district. During one of his trips he was hospitalized in San Francisco and caught the eye of a young nurse. He was about sixty at the time. His marriage to the nurse compelled Lucy to file suit for divorce in Mariposa County Superior Court on September 25, 1899.

Because of John's notoriety and Lucy's daring to file for divorce, the trial made headlines in all the papers from Mariposa to San Francisco. Depending on your outlook, this may have been the first palimony suit in the United States; some would say that the Indian wedding ceremony could not be recognized. In any event, it was unheard of for an Indian woman to use the court system on her own behalf. The newspapers were quick to champion her cause against her millionaire husband, and reporters wrote of her at great length. Judge Corcoran removed himself from the case and called on his good friend, Judge

Joseph J. Jones, of Contra Costa County, who heard the case without a jury. Both sides retained the best lawyers and, as the reader may guess, those working for Lucy were looking to the notoriety the case would bring should they win.

The capacity of the old courtroom was taxed for days with spectators and the press. The suit dragged with legal maneuvers on both sides and a parade of witnesses. When Lucy was asked what was her relationship with John, she said: "I know John Hite. I was married to him a long time ago. I was never married to anyone but John Hite. He said to me, 'Conna me cha; meenee conna longa.' In Indian language, all means 'You are my wife, I am your husband.' I repeated the words, 'Conna me cha.' 'I am your wife.' Hite said, 'Meenee conna longa.' 'I am your husband.' After that, I lived with him as his wife." The attorneys for Lucy called more than one hundred witnesses to testify as to her character and that John had introduced her as his wife to many of them on numerous occasions.

Finally, on December 3, 1899, after days of testimony, the court awarded Lucy fifty dollars a month for the rest of her life and ruled that John was to pay all court costs. Evidently the court did not recognize the possibility of bigamy as there were no charges brought against him. John's appeal to the California Supreme Court was turned away, and Lucy began receiving her "alimony." But this was not the end of the Hite divorce episode.

John Hite had been paying Tom Gibbs, Lucy's son, $100 a month before the court settlement, and now that was cut off. Tom talked his mother into suing for a cash settlement, which she reluctantly did. More lawyers were hired and a suit filed, which hadn't been settled in the court at the end of another year. Finally, when the patience of the court and all those involved was at an end, John and Lucy met in conference at the Grosjean place, southeast of Mariposa. Isolated in a room, they agreed on a settlement. The outcome was that Lucy would receive $21,000 for which she would sign away any rights to John's estate. Of that amount, she would give $5,000 to her four attorneys in payment for their services. The court, probably with a sigh of relief, approved the arrangement over the loud objections of Lucy's lawyers, who felt that each of them was entitled to $5,000.

Lucy gave her son $10,000, which soon was gone. The remaining $6,000 she kept in her trunk, not trusting a bank. She never had a chance to enjoy much of the money. Soon after the settlement, while Lucy was working as a housekeeper, the trunk and its contents were stolen.

Lucy outlived John by nearly twenty years. To the end she maintained she never wanted the money, she just wanted John. She died destitute and a ward of the county—a sad end for a great lady.

As we sit in the picturesque old courtroom and reminisce about the attorneys who established their reputations here and the history that has been made here, we are humbled, to say the least. Here were tried some of the greatest mining disputes of all time. One of them, Biddle Boggs vs. Merced Mining Company, made legal mining history.

John C. Fremont's legal problems involving his Las Mariposas Grant were far from over when he won title to the land in the 1855 decision of the United States Supreme Court. Following the orders of the court, the long irregular strip of land encompassing almost the entire length of Mariposa Creek was thrown out and a survey was ordered to be approved by the surveyor general. Upon receiving the approved survey, Fremont immediately applied to the secretary of the interior for a patent, which was signed by President Pierce on February 19, 1856. Now commenced a series of injunctions, suits, countersuits and legal maneuvers by both sides that created a maze in the courts. It took the best lawyers of the land to untangle who owned what, draining Fremont's mining ventures on the grant of any profit.

Soon after the patent was recorded in the official records at the Mariposa County Courthouse, Fremont's agents began restraining individual miners and secured an injunction against the Merced Mining Company. This company had been operating the Pine Tree, Josephine and Mount Ophir mines under the belief that the land was owned by the public. As you can imagine, Fremont's harassment of the miners was not popular with the citizens and soon the miners were pitted against him. To make matters worse, on April 22, 1857, Fremont leased the Mount Ophir property to Biddle Boggs for a seven-year period at a monthly rental of $1,000. The Merced Mining Company took the issue to the Thirteenth District Court in Mariposa.

Mount Ophir Mill. 1860 Carleton Watkins salt print.

An impressive group of attorneys for both sides was assembled: for Fremont and Boggs, headed by Rufus A. Lockwood, were H. G. Worthington and R. H. Daley of Mariposa, assisted by William T. Wallace (afterwards chief justice), S. Heydenfeldt (former associate justice of the state supreme court), Charles T. Potts, Joseph G. Baldwin (later associate justice of the state supreme court) and D. W. Perly. The attorneys for the Merced Mining Company were Alexander Deering and B. B. Harris, of Mariposa, and Elisha Cook, Gregory Yale, S. W. Fenner of the firm of Cook and Fenner, and the firm of Halleck, Peachy and Billings.

By consent of both parties, a jury was waived and the case was heard before Judge E. Burke in June 1857 at the Mariposa County Courthouse. On July 2 he delivered his opinion—perhaps the most significant decision in the whole history of Mariposa: first, that Fremont's patent was good; second, that Fremont could not be stopped in his insistence that he held legal title; third, that the Merced Mining Company was not entitled to relief; fourth, that Fremont could recover the property held by the Merced Mining Company and recover damages. Of course this was not acceptable to the company so they appealed to the state supreme court.

It should be mentioned that with the granting to Fremont of the title to his land, those on the property banded together to attempt to protect what they thought were their rights. As the trial opened in Judge Burke's court, the little courtroom was crowded with spectators, divided into three groups: neutrals, "Fremonters" and "Merceders." On the wall behind the nine-foot judicial bench was the United States flag with thirty-one stars. Following Judge Burke's favorable decision for Fremont, the hostilities between the two factions boiled up to the point of near warfare.

There were now two suits to come before the January 1858 term of the state supreme court. Fremont's motion to restrain the Merced Mining Company from occupancy of the mines was denied, which virtually recognized the tenure of the portions of the Josephine and Pine Tree mines held by the company. The more important case, Biddle Boggs vs. Merced Mining Company, was the other. The bench was composed of Justices Peter Burnett, David S. Terry and Stephen Field. The court examined two points: whether the titles to the mines embraced by the patent passed to Fremont; and if they did not, if the Merced Mining Company had the right to extract the gold from land held in fee by Fremont.

Burnett delivered the decision, holding that the title to the minerals, the important question, passed from Mexico to the United States. The title would remain there, regardless of the fact that California had become a state and that title was held by an individual.

Boggs, as lessee, and Fremont had only the same right to dig for minerals as any other miner, and could not claim the results of others nor prevent their operations. The right to dig for minerals on private property had not specifically been granted by the United States government, but the right to do so must be presumed. This was not an interpretation of the law but an expression of what the law should be.

Benton Mills. Fremont had this water-powered stamp mill and dam built at Ridley's Ferry on the Merced River in 1858 to crush ore from the Pine Tree and Josephine mines. At one time it had more than sixty stamps.

Judge Terry concurred and Field dissented. Thus Judge Burke's decision was overturned.

A rehearing was scheduled after a vigorous challenge by Fremont's lawyers but did not come up for another year. Two losses handed Fremont by the court strengthened the hand of those in opposition as they expected Fremont's title soon to be dissolved. A mass meeting was held by those in opposition to Fremont where resolutions were drafted denouncing him and asking Congress to set aside his patent to the Las Mariposas. Shortly after, the situation at the Pine Tree boiled over and the "Hornitos League" laid siege on that part called "The Black Drift," which was being worked by Fremont's men. A whole book could be written on this one episode. We will say here that because of Fremont and other calm heads no blood was spilled. However, a whole new round of litigation would tax the seating capacity of this now familiar courtroom in the Mariposa County Courthouse. Here, in district court, a temporary settlement was reached until the state supreme court could re-hear the Biddle Boggs case.

During this wait Fremont pushed ahead in developing a gigantic water-powered quartz mill on the Merced River known as Benton Mills, named for his late father-in-law, Senator Benton. The construction of a railroad connecting the mill with the Pine Tree and Josephine mines was completed. During this time the Pine Tree was turning out gold at the rate of $1,000 a week. Great as that was, it still could not cover expenses for other projects and litigation. Fremont was forced to admit several of his legal advisors into part-ownership of the estate. He still held a controlling interest, but just barely.

The fate of Biddle Boggs vs. Merced Mining Company was settled by a strange turn of events which involved the personnel of the state supreme court. Judge Burnett, who rendered the decision adverse to Fremont in January 1858, resigned, and his place was taken by Joseph J. Baldwin, formerly an attorney in the case. In September 1859, Judge Terry resigned from the bench and shortly thereafter killed politician David C. Broderick in California's most famous duel. His place was taken by W. W. Cope. Stephen J. Field, who had disagreed in the first trial, became the chief justice. Fremont's appeal was heard during the October 1859 session, and amid charges of bribery and corruption on the part of the judges, the final decision in the important case was read on November 15, 1859, by Chief Justice Field. Cope concurred, and Baldwin did not sit on the case.

Field concluded that the only official survey of the estate was that ordered by the United States Supreme Court. Therefore, there could be no grounds for fraud, as the Mariposans had insisted. Ownership of the minerals in the soil would have to wait until the case could be presented to a full bench. However, the Merced Mining Company could not set up claims under the preemption laws, for mineral land was exempted by Congress.

Fremont, by right-of-patent, could enter upon the premises and extract the minerals, as they were granted with the title. Field perceived the United States as holding only the position of a private proprietor having no municipal sovereignty within state limits. In the case of California, the state could only issue a license for a miner to enter lands that were public. Federal legislation was yet to be adopted for either private or public lands.

Fremont, because no one else held license, must be permitted, at the exclusion of all others, to work the mines within the boundaries of his grant. He was the final winner. Not only mining activities would be affected, but also all other interests within his estate. He owned the land, water, buildings, minerals and everything else pertaining to real estate. The decision was contested but was not shaken and, in fact, was strengthened by the 1861 cases of Moore vs. Smaw and Fremont vs. Flower. These cases opened the door for Congress to pass the first federal mining act, in 1866.

The "squatters" were more or less at Fremont's mercy, but early on he demonstrated his willingness to settle equitably. At this time he deeded the property on which the courthouse stood to the county and did not even reserve the mineral rights.

Before we close, we want to ask the reader's consideration of the following: the amount (over four hundred thousand dollars) spent in two restoration projects on the historical Mariposa County Courthouse, to keep alive this structure which was built for $9,200, should serve as a clear demonstration of the pride the residents of the county have in their beloved courthouse. We pray that after reading this book, the reader also will be dedicated to preserving this "Shrine to Justice in California."

The Mariposa Courthouse

There's a little white Courthouse, I'm leaving it soon,
  And somehow it seems hard to go,
For this Courthouse has found a place in my heart,
  I shall miss it always, I know.
For here I have studied and labored and dreamed,
  And hoped for advancement, too,
But, oh, in my triumph I'm dreary just now,
  Goodbye, little Courthouse, to you!

And though I may sit in a courtroom ornate,
  With appointments so modern and fine;
Yet well do I know as now I depart
  I shall miss that old courtroom of mine;
I'll think of its white boarded ceiling and walls,
  The long bench and the clean, polished floor,
And I know that in fancy I'll come back
  To sit in that courtroom once more.

I look from my chambers up into the hills,
  In the distance Mt. Bullion I see;
Through the warm winter sunshine so clear and so bright,
  It seems to beckon to me.
The hills seem so cheery and peaceful and green,
  With a charm one can never forget,
It's the thrill and romance of the old Mother Lode,
  Where the pioneer spirit lives yet.

How stately you stand there amid the green hills,
  A last wistful look and I go,
A century long you've stood there in the sun
  Above the fog in the valley below;
Your famous old clock is just striking twelve,
  Its tall tower points toward the sky,
And the time has come for me to depart,
  So, little white Courthouse, goodbye!

(1953)   by Judge Andrew R. Schottky

83

Significant Dates that Concern the History of the Courthouse

February 18, 1850. Statute passed creating the twenty-seven original counties, Mariposa being the largest containing one-fifth of the total area of the state.

March 31, 1850. First meeting of Court of Sessions governing the county at Agua Fria, the county seat.

September 9, 1850. California admitted to the Union.

November 10, 1851. County seat moved from Agua Fria to the town of Mariposa.

April 7, 1852. Grand jury recommended erection of a courthouse.

June 7, 1852. Court of Sessions set a tax rate of $.25 per $100 assessed valuation for erection of public buildings.

April 21, 1854. Court of Sessions discussed the erection of a courthouse in Mariposa.

June 21, 1854. Plan of P. V. Fox adopted.

July 21, 1854. Contract awarded to P. V. Fox and A. F. Shriver in the amount of $9,000 for the construction of a 40½- by 50½-foot two-story structure; completion date, December 31.

February 12, 1855. Court of Sessions accepted the building at their first meeting of the year; final cost $9,200.

May 14, 1855. First meeting of newly-elected three-member board of supervisors; accepted the courthouse.

September 5, 1860. Title to town block on which courthouse stands conveyed to the county by John C. Fremont. (Deeds Book M, page 45)

March 1, 1861. Board of supervisors awarded bid to A. F. Shriver in the amount of $2,500 for the construction of a brick vault.

September 1866. Cupola and clock added; cost of cupola $275 and cost of clock, less labor of installation, $1,130.35.

September 1879. Court system changed in California; superior court now the county's high court.

July 7, 1884. Board of supervisors awarded bid in the amount of $725 to A. W. Josselyn to build picket fence around the courthouse square.

July 20, 1891. Bid of Charles S. Peck in the amount of $1,800 accepted by board of supervisors for second brick vault to be added to the one built in 1861.

April 10, 1903. Before noon, "Fire" was the cry in the county clerk's office. Soot on fire in boarded-up fireplace soon extinguished with buckets of water.

November 4, 1895. It was ordered that a telephone be installed in the clerk's office, one of six installed in Mariposa by the Sun Set Telephone Company.

July 5, 1900. Contract awarded to L. B. Chenowith to construct an annex containing four offices to the rear of the courthouse.

October 25, 1907. Electric lights installed in the courthouse.

March 5, 1912. Bid awarded to W. A. Scott to renovate interior of the courthouse—clothe and paper the downstairs and paint the courtroom in the amount of $320. This included the graining of all the furniture upstairs and the door and window frames.

March 1, 1926. Bid awarded by board of supervisors to Wm. H. Lowrie in the amount of $1,151. 78 for metal fence around Courthouse Square.

April 21, 1929. Historic marker unveiled in front of the courthouse by the Yosemite Parlor No. 21, Native Sons.

March 31, 1930. Hands stolen from the face of the town clock as an April Fool's joke by students from U.C. Berkeley.

February 7, 1935. Courthouse enlarged with State Emergency Relief Act funds by adding a second story to the 1900 annex and enclosing the breezeway between the two.

February 1947. Stairway to courtroom at right front of building removed. Had been blocked off to public use since 1863.

May 27, 1948. Bid of C. C. Bettencourt, $1,285, accepted by board of supervisors for addition to auditor's office.

April 26, 1954. The chief justice of the State of California, the Honorable Phil S. Gibson, declared the Mariposa County Courthouse a "shrine to justice in California."

May 7-16, 1954. Ten-day celebration commemorating the 100th anniversary of the courthouse and the *Mariposa Gazette*.

October 1954. Plans for addition to courthouse opposed by citizens; new central heating system installed instead.

August 10, 1956. Board of supervisors voted to have an aluminum roof installed. Order rescinded.

March 5, 1957. Law library renovated and furnished and other offices furnished with furniture donated from the eleven counties annexed from Mariposa County.

December 1958. Courthouse recognized as California State Landmark No. 670.

May 11, 1964. Courthouse opened for guided tours.

January 5, 1965. Ohlinger & Jones presented report for restoration of courthouse to maximum use and safety, beginning of long list of projects.

January 19, 1971. New Hall of Records completed.

September 13, 1976. Application made to add courthouse to the National Register of Historic Places. Added in 1977.

June 8-10, 1979. One hundred twenty-fifth anniversary celebration of Mariposa County Courthouse and the *Mariposa Gazette*. Theme: "Heritage of Law and Press 1854-1979."

December 13, 1983. Resolution 83-346 passed establishing Courthouse Temporary Construction Fund.

October 22, 1985. Resolution 85-328 grant application for courthouse restoration project from California Parks and Recreation Facilities Act of 1984. A total of $150,000 received; county added another $40,000.

February 16, 1988. Resolution 88-57 put in place a Courthouse Continuing Maintenance Policy.

May 11, 1988. Courthouse Rededication Ceremony.

November 1, 1988. Resolution 88-536 application for $252,900 grant for further restoration; $253,000 received from the 1988 Proposition 70 funds.

Bibliography

Cossley-Batt, Jill L. *The Last of the California Rangers.* New York and London: Funk & Wagnalls Co., 1928.

Crampton, Charles G. *The Opening of the Mariposa Mining Region, 1849-1859, with Particular Reference to the Mexican Land Grant of John Charles Fremont.* Berkeley, June 13, 1941.

Eccleston, Robert. *Diaries of Robert Eccleston.* The Mariposa Indian War 1850-1851. Salt Lake City: University of Utah Press, 1957.

Fremont, John Charles. *Memoirs of My Life.* Vol. 1. Chicago and New York: Belford, Clarke & Company, 1887.

Mariposa County:
Auditor-Recorder, Official Records. Deeds and Patents, 1854-1863.
Clerk, Board of Supervisors Minutes, 1855-1979.
Court of Sessions Minutes, 1850-1855.
District 13, Court Records, 1855-1879.
Superior Court Records, 1880-1910.

Mariposa Museum and History Center, Inc., Mariposa, California. Research Library and Files.

Newspapers:
Gazette-Mariposan, 1901-1905.
Mariposa Chronicle, January 1854-March 1855.
Mariposa Gazette, July 12, 1855-December 1979.
Mariposa Miner, 1934-1939, incl.
San Joaquin Republican, Stockton, 1851.
Stockton Times, 1850.

Pinkerton, Scott. Personal files. Mariposa, California.

Spence, Mary Lee. *The Expeditions of John Charles Fremont.* Vol. 3. Urbana and Chicago: University of Illinois Press, 1984.

Index

Page numbers in italic print indicate pictures or illustrations.